The Adventure of Faith

When Religion is Just the Beginning

John Luongo

They that hope in the Lord will
renew their strength,
they will soar as with eagles' wings;
They will run and not grow weary,
walk and not grow faint.

Isaiah 40:31

PAULIST PRESS
New York and Mahwah, N.J.

Book design by Nighthawk Design.

Library of Congress Cataloging-in-Publication Data

Luongo, John, 1941–
    The adventure of faith: when religion is just the beginning/by John
Luongo.
        p. cm.
    ISBN 0-8091-3313-X (pbk.)
    1. Spiritual life—Catholic authors. I. Title.
BX2350.7.L86 1992
248.4′82—dc20   92-15128
                                                                  CIP

Published by Paulist Press
997 Macarthur Boulevard
Mahwah, New Jersey 07430

Printed and bound in the
United States of America

CONTENTS

Prologue   vii

Part One: Assessing Your Experience
of Religion and Spirituality

1 Introduction   3

2 What's the Difference Between Religion and
    Spirituality?   7

3 What Motivates You To Respond to God?   10

4 What Can You Do To Enhance Your Spirituality?   17

Part Two: Getting Started

5 Are You *Listening* to the Bible as the Word of
    God?   29

6 Are You Experiencing Grace as *Power*?   35

7 What Effect Is Culture Having on Your
    Responses to God?   39

Part Three: Signs of Life

8 Are You Searching for Truth?   45

9 Are You Free from External Coercion?   48

10 Are You Free from Internal Coercion?   50

11   Is Your Relationship with Jesus Sufficiently
       Personal?   54

12   Are You Contributing to the Life of the Church?   60

13   Is Your Growth Harmonious and Integral?   70

14   Is Your Sacramental Life "*Sign*-ificant?"   74

Part Four: Christian Transformations

15   Fixed Ideology or Insight?   85

16   Observation or Contemplation?   92

17   Security or Openness?   98

18   "The Answer" or Questions?   104

19   Pleasure or Meaning?   112

20   Externals or Internals?   118

21   Attachment or Commitment?   126

22   Compulsion or Gifts?   133

23   Captivity or Freedom?   140

24   Illusions or Truth?   144

25   Pride or Relationship?   149

26   Alienation or Unity?   154

27   Conclusion   159

Appreciations

I am grateful to all those who helped me complete this book. To those who encouraged me while I wrote: Pat and Karen Cardinale, Mike and Pat Collins, Rosemary Archer, Marlene Paulson, and Joe and Margo Bollich. To Al and Ardy Smetona for my photograph, to Frank Lojacono for guiding me through the process of getting the "permissions," and to Patty Broesamle for encouraging me to submit the manuscript to Paulist Press. And to Doug Fisher, who was the editor.

* * *

ACKNOWLEDGMENTS

Paulist Press gratefully acknowledges use of: Excerpts from the English translation of *Rite of Baptism for Children* 1969, International Committee on English in the Liturgy, Inc.; *Vatican Council II, Conciliar and Post-Conciliar Documents* Copyright © 1975, 1984, 1987, 1988, 1992 by Rev. Austin Flannery, O.P. Permissions for extractions from this edition administered by Costello Publishing Company, Inc., P.O. Box 9, Northport, N.Y. 11768, USA.; *To Have or To Be* by Erich Fromm. HarperCollins, NY, NY.; *Motivation and Personality* by Abraham H. Maslow. Harper-Collins, NY, NY.; *Conjectures of a Guilty Bystander* by Thomas Merton. Doubleday, Dell Publishing Group, NY, NY.; Scripture selections are taken from the *New American Bible* copyright © 1970 by the Confraternity of Christian Doctrine, Washington, D.C., and the *Revised New Testament of the New American Bible*, copyright © 1986 by the CCD are used by license of the copyright owner. All rights reserved. No part of the *New American Bible* or the *Revised New Testament* may be used or reproduced in any form, without permission in writing from the copyright owner; *Psycho-Cybernetics* by Maxwell Maltz. Simon and Schuster, Englewood Cliffs, N.J. 1960, 1988; *The New Man* by Thomas Merton. Copyright © 1961 by the Abbey of Gethsemani. Renewal copyright © 1989 by the Trustees of the Merton Legacy Trust. Reprinted by permission of Farrar, Straus & Giroux, Inc.; *New Seeds of Contemplation* by Thomas Merton. Copyright © 1961 by The Abbey of Gethsemani, Inc., New Directions, NY, NY.

DEDICATION

This book is dedicated to military chaplains, and to the people of God whom they serve throughout the world. I am proud to have shared in this unique ministry during my career as a U.S. Air Force chaplain, and I am eternally grateful to the late Most Rev. William R. Johnson, founding Bishop of the Diocese of Orange in California, for giving me this privilege.

PROLOGUE

My purpose in writing this book is to look at the church with youthful naiveté, to dream about what could be . . . about a church in which *all* of the sacraments serve as powerful signs of the counter-cultural nature of Christianity . . . about a church that is characterized by a youthful sense of curiosity and adventure.

It grieves me to watch parishioners simply repeat what they learned as children with little or no analytical thought, or with minimal involvement in a community of faith. I am certain that God wants each of his children to keep growing and to keep sharing personal gifts forever; this is what communion, love, and heaven are all about. For adults or children, the essence of being childlike in a creative, spiritual manner never changes: it is to use Christian freedom as a catalyst to convert playfulness, trust, curiosity, and even elements of *fear* into spiritual growth and renewal.

Baptism is meant to serve as the beginning of the unique growth process that takes place within Christian communities. This uniqueness is the result of the synergy (our combined total is greater than the sum of our individual contributions) that is attributable to "grace." When creative, life-giving people inter-act with others in the network of relationships we call "commu-nity," their energy, curiosity, and enthusiasm help facilitate an exchange of gifts that produces a lifetime of growth and re-newal. Christian spirituality is the result of sustained efforts to discover the unique truthfulness and creativity that characterize "graced" relationships with God.

Because spiritual growth and renewal are the church's "vital signs," my second purpose is to shift perceptions of baptism from cleansing toward *rebirth*. There are two reasons for this adjustment:

1. Since belief in Christ's resurrection lies at the core of our faith, we ought to emphasize it—especially in the ritual that initiates newcomers. Paragraph 6 of the General Introduction of the *Rite of Catholic Baptism for Children* does. "Those who are baptized are engrafted in the likeness of Christ's death. They are buried with him, they are given life again with him, and with him they rise again."

2. In Greek, *"baptisma"* refers to the process of dipping under, the experience of immersion or plunging. *Baptism means immersion*—into the water to symbolize suffering and death, and out of the water to symbolize resurrection. Baptism "by immersion" is redundant.

This conceptual shift suggests a change of method too; thus, paragraph 22 of the General Introduction of the *Rite of Catholic Baptism for Children* describes the rite of *immersion* as ". . . more suitable [than the pouring of water] as a symbol of participation in the death and resurrection of Christ. . . ."

This book is not meant to serve as a catechism—it is about the spiritual process that begins with baptism. Its purpose is to add methodology to your theology, and to help you to keep asking questions that lead toward spiritual growth. It is about the experience of generosity and the creative application of freedom; its focus is on the experience of God, neighbor and self in a vigorous experience of church.

1. Chapters 1 to 14 contain a framework made up of questions and graphics that you can use to assess the intensity of

your spiritual life. Testing the effects of your decisions will help you to understand how the experience of spirituality complements religion, how spirituality leads to emotional well-being and personal growth, and how the sacraments *"sign"*-ify the process of our conversion.

2. Chapters 15 to 26 present twelve transformations that can help you to fulfill the promise of baptism. Each of the twelve reflects one aspect of the contrast between salvation and sin and death, or between faith and anxiety, or between prayer and complacency.

You may use these tools for a self-analysis of personal spirituality and to develop your own methodical approach to spiritual growth and renewal. Keep in mind that the church is uniquely able to provide an environment that facilitates spiritual growth and adventure—because Christ and the Holy Spirit provide them.

John the Baptist, the prophet who served as the link between the *old* covenant and the eternal *new*ness of life in the Spirit, began his ministry by recalling Isaiah's words:

I am "the voice of one crying out in the desert,
Make straight the way of the Lord . . ." (Jn 1:23).

Making straight "the way of the Lord" means being motivated to communicate as prophets: (1) the value of prayerful openness to the word of God, (2) the necessity of sharing God's gifts, and (3) the joy which flows from the attainment of spiritual unity.

As you read, keep in mind that the purpose of your baptism (or the baptism of your dependent children) is to create new life in the body of Christ, a life that embodies the hope and strength that Isaiah described nearly twenty-seven hundred years ago:

> They that hope in the Lord will renew their strength,
>   they will soar as with eagles' wings;
> They will run and not grow weary,
>   walk and not grow faint (Is 40:31).

Take a few moments to review the Contents. If you try to respond openly to the questions that the following chapters will raise, the Lord will keep renewing your strength too.

Part One

Assessing Your Experience
of Religion and Spirituality

CHAPTER ONE

Introduction

Judging mostly on outward appearance, most people probably regard me as a "religious" person. The evidence seems to support their perception. In 1974, at the age of thirty-three, I resigned from a secure and rewarding career with IBM to enter a seminary; I have been a priest since 1978.

The externals of human behavior do not necessarily portray an accurate picture. Over the years my responses to God have been changing dramatically. Instead of obeying laws out of fear of God's punishment, I am learning how to use the sacraments as expressions of "graced" partnerships with God and neighbor. What I was taught as a child focused primarily on learning how to be "good"; what I have learned to value—and what I will focus on in this book—is how to respond to the goodness of God.

The transformation that has occurred beneath the surface of my behavior is the result of a decision-making process that is helping me to convert problems into opportunities to grow. The major events in my life (such as ordination to the priesthood) are merely milestones; they are not as significant as the decisions I make each day in the struggle to use God's grace to deal with the effects of sin. I am optimistic about this for two reasons. First, grace is free for the asking. Second, the problems that cause my greatest anxieties also reveal just how well I am using my freedom to respond to God.

FIGURE 1.1   DEALING WITH SUFFERING

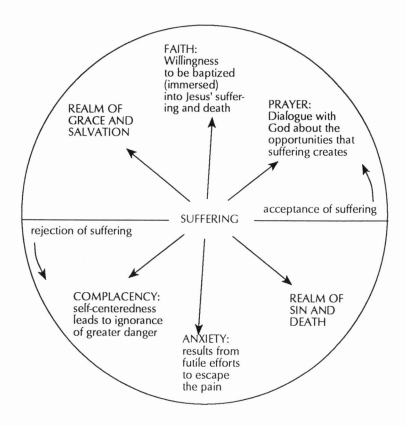

FAITH:
Willingness
to be baptized
(immersed)
into Jesus' suffer-
ing and death

PRAYER:
Dialogue with
God about the
opportunities that
suffering creates

REALM OF
GRACE AND
SALVATION

acceptance of suffering

SUFFERING

rejection of suffering

COMPLACENCY:
self-centeredness
leads to ignorance
of greater danger

ANXIETY:
results from
futile efforts
to escape
the pain

REALM OF
SIN AND
DEATH

Since problems don't go away by themselves, and since they can't be thrown out like garbage, we might as well learn how to accept them. Figure 1.1 depicts the opposite extremes that we may take when faced with pain and suffering. Notice that the opposite of prayer is complacency (ignorance of danger), not "no prayer," and that the opposite of faith is anxiety, not "no faith." Most of all, notice that the opposite of salvation is death, and that *the purpose of baptism is to commit ourselves to a lifestyle that transforms suffering and death into a "graced" way of life.* See Figure 1.1.

The greater our daily effort to "relate" to Jesus, the more we will be "graced"; conversely, movement away from God leads into the realm of sin and death. Because sin is a decision to move *away* from a relationship with God, it is a matter of choosing death instead of life, and the root cause of poor spiritual health. When we become complacent, or when we are paralyzed by the anxieties that accompany problems, we are allowing sin and death to ensnare us. The signs of complacency and anxiety abound: the almost universal tendency of institutions and individuals to "pass the buck," drug-abuse—to cover up the pain that problems bring, and the poor self-images that people use to punish themselves.

The institutional model of church that I accepted as a child distracted my attention from the experience of Jesus as a *person*. This distraction was largely the result of "bureaucracy." Because of their size, all large institutions, including the church, create certain difficulties for their members. Behavioral scientists refer to the negative behaviors that result as "bureaupathological." While this term may sound harsh, it is simply a description of the harmful or "pathological" side-effects that bureaucracies have on the behavior of their members. In this case, the harmful side-effect was that religion, a means to the end of a personal relationship with Jesus, became instead an end in itself.

The purpose of this book is to help you to ask questions that serve as incentives for the spiritual growth and renewal that flow out of a healthy relationship with Jesus; Chapters 1 to 14 lay the foundation for this. Chapters 15–26 then present a series of twelve spiritual transformations; the goal for each transformation is highlighted in italics above the dotted line on the right hand side of Table 1.1. The first decision, which is the subject of Chapter 15, is whether to accept "insight" or a fixed ideology.

Table 1.1 *Framework for Analysis*

Concept	Context	Catalyst	Goals for Each of the Twelve Transformations			
Salvation	(Being liberated by God)	Integration:	*Freedom* 9	*Truth* 10	*Relationship* 11	*Unity* 12
Faith	(Placing God's will above own)	Action:	*Meaning* 5	*Internals* 6	*Commitment* 7	*Gifts* 8
Prayer	(Dialoguing with God)	The exchange:	*Questions* 4	*Insight* 1	*Contemplation* 2	*Openness* 3
			|	|	|	|
			Seek?	Accept?	Respond?	Express?
			< -- >			
			Transformations—decisions to:			

On the horizontal plane, notice how salvation (being liberated by God) is made up of an ongoing integration of decisions that relate to freedom, truth, relationship, and unity. On the vertical dimension, notice how salvation builds on faith, and faith on prayer.

Before we can effectively evaluate our motives for responding to Jesus, and the steps we can take to enhance our spirituality, we will have to deal with some of the obstacles that can get in the way. Ironically, some of these obstacles are related to religion.

CHAPTER TWO

What's the Difference Between Religion and Spirituality?

When questioned about their *relationship* with God, most Roman Catholics tend to speak in terms of being or not being "religious." In this context, being "religious" is the equivalent of whatever being "a good Catholic" means. The purpose of this chapter is to explain why religion may become an obstacle to spiritual growth.

There is nothing wrong with religion if it is balanced by the active spiritual life that makes baptism a sacrament. The problems begin when religion is allowed to stifle the creative, open-ended process called "spirituality." This occurs because of the unusual way that our brain works: while it functions as a whole, each half has a distinct purpose and mode of operating. Table 2.1 summarizes the differences:

Table 2.1 *How our Brain Functions*

Left Half of Brain	Right Half of Brain
orderly	creative
tends to look more outside self	looks more deeply inside self
takes apart, looks at details	sees the whole all at once
verbal	non-verbal
rational	intuitive

The right side of the brain controls the left side of our body, and the left side of our brain controls the right side of our body. In general, the educational system in the United States is biased toward the production of right-handed, left-brained thinkers.

Since left-brain thinking favors religion over spirituality, it takes extra will power to accept the risks and rewards associated with spirituality. Table 2.2 summarizes them.

Table 2.2   *Religion and Spirituality*

Left Half of Brain	Right Half of Brain
Values the structure and *order* of religion	Values the *creative* power of spirituality
Values the *external* standards that provide a sense of law and order	Values the experience of an *indwelling* Holy Spirit
Dissects sacraments into *detailed parts* with minimal emphasis on their context	Sees the sacraments in their *whole* context (to mirror the story of salvation history)
Places more emphasis on saying the right *words*	Values the graphic *non-verbal* dimension of the sacraments (e.g. baptism as immersion)
Uses *thought* to control behavior by emphasizing and enforcing rules and laws	Uses *intuition* to embrace the prophetical and mystical dimensions of faith

Table 2.3 highlights five key benefits associated with spiritual life; these conversions describe the essence of Christian life.

Table 2.3   *Spirituality as Conversion*

From:	To:
knowledge of facts	internalization of meaning
law and order	expression of gifts
God as punitive	God as life-giver/enabler
church as they/pyramid	church as me/us
salvation as saving my soul	salvation as one's life shared with God and neighbor

These conversions have modest beginnings. Long before we can begin to grasp what God expects from us, we have a good idea of what we want from God. The next chapter will arrange our motives for responding to God in a hierarchy that begins with religion and ends with spirituality.

CHAPTER THREE

What Motivates You To Respond to God?

The purpose of this chapter is to study the hierarchy of motives that lead beyond religiosity to spirituality:

SPIRITUAL UNITY WITH GOD AND NEIGHBOR

MYSTERY AND ADVENTURE

QUESTIONS

REWARDS AND PUNISHMENTS

PROBLEM-SOLVING

Beginning with problem-solving, as each need is satisfied, another emerges—drawing us ever closer to God and one another. Collectively, these needs serve as the driving force behind our responses to God; they do so by providing the motivation we need to sustain our spiritual growth.

Let's start at the bottom. At one time or another, most of us are tempted to bargain with God by offering to do or not do something in exchange for a particular favor: "If you get me out of this mess, I'll. . . ." You can probably provide your own examples. See Figure 3.1.

There are several things wrong with this type of relationship. First, if God solved all our problems, we would be deprived of

FIGURE 3.1 PROBLEMS

Take my problem away! (motive)

Turn to God?

opportunities that we need to grow, and our behavioral patterns would be substantially the same as animals who are "trained" to perform for their handlers. Second, we tend to forget promises made under duress. In short, this type of "motivation" is fundamentally immature. It is both unjust and unhealthy for us to attempt to use God as just a problem-solver.

In the absence of urgent problems, our motivation to have relationship with God usually shifts to getting rewards or avoiding punishment. See Figure 3.2.

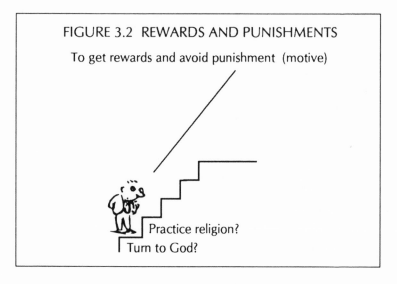

FIGURE 3.2 REWARDS AND PUNISHMENTS

To get rewards and avoid punishment (motive)

Practice religion?
Turn to God?

To get the reward or avoid the punishment, we agree to practice religion by engaging in one or more of the following types of activities:

1. membership in a particular denomination
2. acceptance of specific teachings and beliefs
3. attending rituals

If taking the step of practicing religion never goes beyond these three activities, we will not grow to full stature. God will not punish us for being "bad," but we will suffer from the negative effects associated with complacency or anxiety; therefore, it is in our best interest to carry our search further.

Our next motive has to do with asking questions about the meaning and purpose of human life. See Figure 3.3.

At this level, using the practice of religion as a stepping stone, we must decide whether or not to enter into a dialogue with God about our needs and values, and the needs and values of others; the book of Job provides a good illustration. Once we decide to

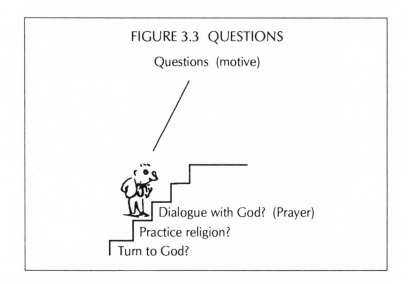

FIGURE 3.3 QUESTIONS

Questions (motive)

Dialogue with God? (Prayer)

Practice religion?

Turn to God?

take the step of entering into a dialogue with God, we have begun to make the transition that leads beyond religion to spirituality.

Unless we sustain this prayerful dialogue with God, the quality of our spiritual life will inevitably suffer. Similarly, as the rewards and punishments that served as the motivation to practice religion fade, we may be tempted to regress by giving up the practice of religion until another serious problem arises. Therefore, using both the practice of religion and prayer as stepping stones, we can uncover yet another motive: to enter into the sense of mystery and adventure that Jesus embodies in his person. See Figure 3.4.

At this level, building on the stepping stones of religion and prayer, and motivated by the mystery and adventure that Jesus embodies, we must decide whether to place God's will above our own. *This is the decisive step that expresses faith; the most appropriate ritual is baptism, which graphically expresses a commitment to suffer and die with Jesus.*

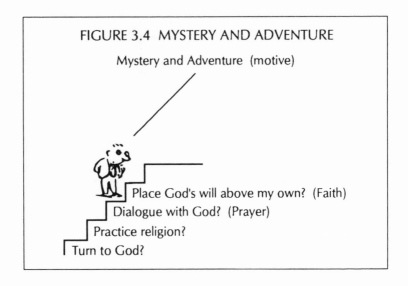

FIGURE 3.4 MYSTERY AND ADVENTURE

Mystery and Adventure (motive)

Place God's will above my own? (Faith)
Dialogue with God? (Prayer)
Practice religion?
Turn to God?

Until we are motivated enough to keep taking the risks that flow from submitting to God's will and being *participants* in the mystery and adventure of faith, we are quite vulnerable to complacency and anxiety. The danger is twofold: that the questions that have served as the motivation to search for truth will eventually become stale, or that anxiety will begin to compel us to seek "the" answer instead. Therefore, building on the stepping stones of religion, prayer, and faith, we can now consider the highest human motive—to achieve spiritual unity with God and neighbor. See Figure 3.5.

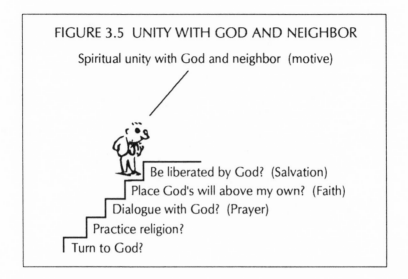

FIGURE 3.5 UNITY WITH GOD AND NEIGHBOR

Spiritual unity with God and neighbor (motive)

Be liberated by God? (Salvation)
Place God's will above my own? (Faith)
Dialogue with God? (Prayer)
Practice religion?
Turn to God?

At this level, motivation shifts from mystery and adventure to achieving spiritual unity with God and neighbor. Since we are social by nature, this ought to be a powerful motive; unfortunately, because of original sin, satisfying our need for spiritual unity is intrinsically difficult. *Taking this last step—of choosing to be liberated by God—is contingent on maintaining openness as we dialogue with him, and on being willing to keep submitting to his will as we continue to grow in insight.*

God liberates those who seek him and are willing to submit to his will by empowering them with spiritual gifts. These gifts, which result from the integration of freedom, truth, relationship, and unity, form a unique bond that cannot be broken. See Figure 3.6. (Chapters 4 and 23–26 explain this process in detail.)

Notice that the practice of religion forms the stepping stone for the experience of prayer, faith, and salvation.

FIGURE 3.6 SALVATION AS FREEDOM, TRUTH,
RELATIONSHIP, UNITY

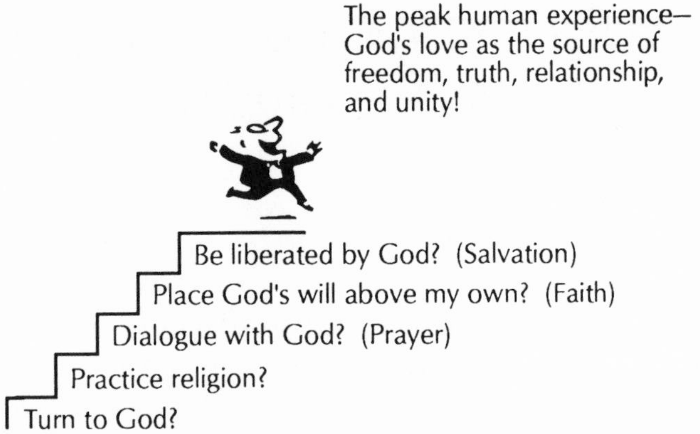

The peak human experience—
God's love as the source of
freedom, truth, relationship,
and unity!

Be liberated by God? (Salvation)
Place God's will above my own? (Faith)
Dialogue with God? (Prayer)
Practice religion?
Turn to God?

Salvation is a spiritual liberation. Unlike the ancient Israelites who were freed from captivity to Pharaoh, God has freed us from sin and death! It's a gift we can neither earn nor repay. By the grace of God we can become his heirs, his adopted children, living temples of his Spirit. "Praised be the God and Father of our Lord Jesus Christ, who has bestowed on us every spiritual blessing in the heavens" (Eph 1:3). Keep Paul's advice to "acquire a fresh, spiritual way of thinking" (Eph 4:23) in mind— because many of the "problems" that we bring to God are symptoms of *spiritual* "dis-ease." And remember that religious activities are not ends in themselves; their purpose is to promote and facilitate spiritual life.

The next chapter will build on the above motives by providing ten specific suggestions you can use to enhance your experience of spiritual life.

CHAPTER FOUR

What Can You Do To Enhance Your Spirituality?

Most people tend to see authority to act in the church as flowing downward from the top of a pyramid. However, as the power of the Holy Spirit is actualized by individual Christians, authority to act becomes more diffuse. It might even be argued that authority flows from the bottom up through the consent of those who have literally chosen to be "affiliated" with God by becoming adopted sons and daughters.

One problem with seeing all authority as flowing downward is that the more organized a religion becomes, the greater the risk that good intentions will be translated into teachings and beliefs that, once committed to memory, allow people to feel comfortable *as they are.* Until we have completed our life's journey, such comfort is premature. Thomas Merton expressed the danger in these words in *Conjectures of a Guilty Bystander:*

> Man "wishes himself" (magically) to become godly, holy, gentle, pure. His wish terminates not in God but in himself. This is no more than the religion of those who wish themselves to be in a certain state in which they can live with themselves, approve of themselves: for they feel that, when they approve of themselves, God is at peace with them. How many Christians seriously believe that Christianity is nothing more than this? Yet it is anathema to true Christianity.

The whole meaning of Paul's anger with "the Law" and with "the elements of this world" is seen here. Such religion is not saved by good intentions: in the end it becomes a caricature. It must. For otherwise we would never see the difference between this and the "religion" which perhaps ought not to be called religion, born from the devastation of our trivial "self" and all our plans for "our self," even though they be plans for a holy self, a pure self, a loving sacrificing self.

I have been using the term "spirituality" to refer to the experience that Merton describes as ". . . the 'religion' which perhaps ought not to be called religion, born from the devastation of our trivial self. . . ." I am certain that Merton's objection was directed toward what I have been describing as "religiosity." Merton did not intend to disparage the importance of religion, and neither do I.

The more Spirit-filled a person becomes, the less room is left for what Merton called "our trivial self." The church as the body of Christ cannot achieve its potential unless we, its individual members, are transformed from "trivial selves" into temples of the Holy Spirit. Diffusion of authority in the church is a necessity because it serves as a "vital sign" of the spiritual health of both the individual and the comm*unity.*

The comparison of religiosity and spirituality that follows is an imperfect attempt to describe the characteristics of spiritual growth. Each comparison will be summarized by a principle that describes an essential quality of life in the Spirit.

The first characteristic of spirituality is that its emphasis is on unity, e.g. community, communion, etc. Wherever the power of the Holy Spirit is actualized, there is sure to be action in gatherings that are characterized by "fellowship" and that also give communal thanks and praise to God. Catholic and Anglican religious communities provide a good example of the variety of communal forms that spirituality may take. Communities made up of lay people within a large parish or congregation manifest the dynamism of the Holy Spirit in a similar manner. In contrast, religion places more emphasis on form, for example, on uniformity. Form certainly plays a necessary role by providing the stability, predictability, and identity that allow participants to feel secure—especially in worship and rituals. The importance of being sensitive to the need for form becomes clear because of the large numbers of Catholics who dropped out of the church when English replaced Latin at mass. **First principle: God wants us to cooperate with the Holy Spirit to unify the church.**

The second characteristic of spirituality is that its message is embodied by a living person—Jesus Christ, who is God's Word made flesh. Jesus dwells in each believer through his Spirit, the Paraclete, the Spirit of truth; by making a personal response to Jesus and thereby receiving the Holy Spirit, we can experience God's truth from within. On the other hand, the messages that religion presents are carefully defined by specific teachings and beliefs that fall under the headings of doctrine, dogma, and law. These too play a necessary role by providing uniformity, along with stability, predictability, and a sense of identity—but they are not, and have never been, literally embodied by Jesus. **Second principle: focus your attention on a personal relationship with Jesus.**

The third characteristic of spirituality is that through contemplation we can begin to penetrate the mystery of faith. People with healthy spiritual lives think—and grow. I'm amazed at how reluctant people are to think about God; as we mature, we ought to experience greater and greater insight. The danger that arises out of religion's emphasis on *teaching* is that insight is not likely to occur when religious instruction is associated primarily with childhood and CCD. Knowledge gained from this limited experience is no substitute for a contemplative relationship with Christ. **Third principle: spend enough time in con-templation, at least once a week, to do some deep thinking about God.**

The fourth characteristic of spirituality is that through the indwelling of the Holy Spirit, God provides the believer with an internal source of power. It has often been said that the road to hell is paved with good intentions. The Spirit-filled Christian has both good intentions and the power needed to act them out. This power is simultaneously the cause and effect of "grace," and its supply is infinite because it comes directly from God. No matter how good a teacher of religion is, the doctrines, dogmas, and laws always remain "externals." They are "externals" be-cause they cannot exist within a person in the same manner that the Holy Spirit does. **Fourth principle: experience God's pres-ence from within—use the grace-power that flows out of your baptismal commitment to suffer and die with Jesus.**

The fifth characteristic of spirituality has to do with the giving and receiving of gifts. The person who is Spirit-filled does not simply obey laws under a sense of obligation—even the ten commandments. Instead, his or her relationships with God and neighbor are characterized by a dynamic exchange of the gifts of the Holy Spirit, an exchange that takes place spontaneously in Christian communities. Such people are especially alert to opportunities to give others whatever they need. In short, what is internal (the Holy Spirit) is exposed to others through the sharing of gifts. In contrast, religion's doctrines, dogmas, and laws influence behavior from the outside in—"what is external is imposed." Unless these rules are seen as mere guidelines, they are likely to cause legalistic behavior—"what do I have to do to get by?" **Fifth principle: be bold and generous in developing and sharing your gifts, and help others to do the same.**

The sixth characteristic of spirituality is action. There's a say-ing that "if you want something done, ask a busy person."

Spirit-filled people get "involved." Their lives are productive and rewarding since they are committed enough to share their Christian gifts with others. In contrast, people who cling to religious practice out of habit are far more likely to be passive. Although their knowledge of doctrines, dogmas, and laws may help them to distinguish between right and wrong, only the Holy Spirit can give them the power to do what is right. **Sixth principle: don't just attend church, help build a community.**

The seventh characteristic of spirituality is commitment and conviction. Spirit-filled Christians use rituals properly to renew their commitments and deepen their convictions. They do not usually arrive late, or leave early. When they go back to their homes and jobs, they bring their commitments and convictions with them and allow Christ, who is the "light of the world" (Jn 8:12; Lk 11:33–36), to shine—despite their imperfections. In contrast, people who consider themselves "religious" are often willing to settle for the comfortable feelings arising from treating rituals as ends in themselves. Good feelings are only one component of a healthy and fulfilling relationship with God; they are not substitutes for faith, commitment, or spiritual growth. **Seventh principle: allow others to see your faith and trust in God by being willing to put His will above your own.**

The eighth characteristic of spirituality is ministry. Spirit-filled Christians take their roles as members of the body of Christ seriously. They do not treat ministry as a job for those who have been ordained. They appreciate that by virtue of baptism they have already made a commitment to continue Jesus' ministry on earth. By refusing to become too dependent on "professional" ministers, they learn to help each other like members of a successful athletic team. It matters less to them who gets the credit than it does to win at spreading "the good news to all creation." (Mk 16:15b). On the other end of the spectrum between religion and spirituality are those who are content to allow church officials to dominate. The highly centralized decision-making process that results tends to encourage passivity and a tendency to blame "them" (the decision makers) for the problems that inevitably arise. **Eighth principle: be a minister.** (You do not have to be ordained to serve others.)

The ninth characteristic of spirituality is tied to behavior that is creative. Christians who actualize the power of the Holy Spirit and who use it to deal with life's problems increase their freedom enormously—because they are more likely to accept pain and suffering and relate it to the cross. Because Spirit-filled Christians are also committed to be life-giving to others, they are never without opportunities to focus their energy on meaningful goals. In contrast, the security that religion provides often produces behavior that is primarily imitative. "Follow these rules and conform to these role-expectations and you will be rewarded." This is the credo of the so-called "organization man." The problem with this type of behavior is that it is too self-centered. **Ninth principle: be life-giving and creative— use God's grace-power to develop personal relationships, and use them to pass on your zest for spiritual life to others.**

The tenth characteristic of spirituality is growth and renewal. Spirit-filled Christians question, evaluate, and update what they have been taught, and are therefore better able to control their own feelings. They are not threatened when others question them, or their particular denominational beliefs. Unfortunately, a systematic study of church history will uncover far too many examples of defensive reactions. To protect yourself from making repetitious and thoughtless responses to God, be a participant in adult education and read theological books and magazines with a critical mind. Take time for contemplation to avoid the repetitious behavior that can result from concepts of life that are primarily taught and felt. If you do not, the obstacles that result from rigid "lessons" and pre-programmed feelings can retard your spiritual growth. These obstacles, whether self-imposed or imposed by others, can be overcome by grace. Thought, grace-power, freedom, and creativity are the major components of the spiritual growth-process that produces balanced and successful lives. **Tenth principle: keep reviewing and updating what you have learned about God and spiritual life.**

Use Table 4.1 to summarize the comparisons made in this chapter. *Cover the right hand column, and read down the left column first to determine how well the description of "religion" fits your experience. Then uncover the right column, and compare each of the eight categories one by one.* Finally, decide for yourself whether your experience of God falls predominantly under the heading of religion or spirituality. Remember, religion is not "bad," it is the foundation for actions that characterize healthy spiritual lives.

Spirituality is a "graced" experience, and grace is power. Since the source of this power is Jesus, the pivotal question in Part Two is: Are you *listening* to the Word of God?

Table 4.1   *The Effects of Religion and Spirituality*

Religion:	Spirituality:
1. Is *institutional:* form is emphasized, e.g. uniformity.	1. Is *communal:* unity is emphasized, e.g. community, communion.
2. The message is carefully *written* in doctrines, dogmas and laws.	2. The message is *embodied* in a living person—God's Word made flesh.
3. Doctrines, dogmas, and laws are *observed.*	3. The mystery that Jesus embodies is gradually penetrated by *contemplation.*
4. No matter how hard you study doctrine, dogma, and law, they remain *"externals"* because they cannot become part of your being.	4. The indwelling presence of the Holy Spirit provides an *"internal"* source of power.
5. *"What is external is imposed."* When obligations define your relationships with God and neighbor, the result is often "what do I have to do to get by?" This is legalism.	5. *"What is internal is exposed."* The person who is Spirit-filled is not bound by obligations. Instead, relationships with God and neighbor are expressed by a dynamic exchange of gifts —the gifts of the Holy Spirit. The result is "what can I give you?"
6. Responses are somewhat *passive.* Although "externals," e.g. laws, can help you to distinguish between right and wrong, they cannot give you the power to do what is right.	6. Responses are more *active* —the indwelling presence of the Holy Spirit is God's guarantee of enough power to do what is right.

Table 4.1 *The Effects of Religion and Spirituality (Continued)*

Religion:	Spirituality:
7. In the absence of power, felt responses tend to become predominant. These *feelings* usually result from merely attending rituals and from careful observance of detail.	7. *Commitment* becomes the predominant response. It is expressed by active participation in rituals (the meaning of the sacramental symbols is internalized and accepted).

8. In the *institutional* model of church:
  (a) *officials* are dominant
  (b) security is tied to behavior that is *imitative*; freedom is restrained.
  (c) *T.A. "Parent"* (taught) *and "Child"* (felt) ego states are prevalent.
  (d) God is often an object of *fear*.
	8. In the *dynamic* models of the church:
	  (a) *ministry* dominates
	  (b) security is tied to behavior that is *creative*; freedom is actualized.
	  (c) *T.A. "Adult"* (thought) ego state is prevalent
	  (d) God is the source of *love*.

Part Two

Getting Started

CHAPTER FIVE

Are You *Listening* to the Bible as the Word of God?

The purpose of this chapter is to consider the prophetic role that Jesus plays as God's Word made flesh. He is God's personal communication link with mankind, the source of love, and the means by which we live and grow in communion with one another in the church.

> In the beginning was the Word;
> the Word was in God's presence,
> and the Word was God.
> Through him all things came into being,
> and apart from him nothing came to be.
> The Word became flesh
> and made his dwelling among us,
> and we have seen his glory:
> the glory of an only Son coming from the Father,
> filled with enduring love (Jn 1:1, 3, 14).

God's Word was embodied in human flesh to deliver a personal message of love, to give us freedom and truth, and to call us to relationship and unity.

Theologians call what God transmits and communicates to us "revelation." Revelation is simply God's input to us, and theol-

ogy is faith seeking understanding. If you are trying to understand how to respond to Jesus as God's communication link
now, *you* are a theologian.

Although God's Word provides answers to life's problems,
his answers all are not heard when they are obscured by the
"static" that surrounds us in everyday life or when our "re-
ceivers" are tuned to other channels.

What God is communicating through Christ is the radical
freedom that lies at the heart of the gospel. This freedom has
always been difficult to accept because it must be preceded by a
commitment to an immersion (the literal meaning of baptism
has to do with dipping or plunging) into Jesus' suffering and
death. In this context, immersion means acceptance of our suffering, not because it is good in itself, but because it is the means
by which we enter into communion with the crucified Jesus, and
the risen Christ. What we call "the cross" has always been the
stumbling block: "The message of the cross is complete absur-
dity to those who are headed for ruin, but to us who are experiencing salvation it is the power of God" (1 Cor 1:18).

Those who refuse to make or fulfill baptismal commitments
face two immediate dangers. The first is that they may become
depressed (angry with themselves) for being unable to cope with
their suffering (because it has no meaning or purpose). The
second is that they may try to cover up the pain with pleasure. In
the extreme, they may even turn to drugs that offer immediate
surges of immense pleasure, but inevitably produce a captivity
that is the polar opposite of the freedom won for us by Christ.

Reading the Bible serves as a prelude to the experience of
Christian freedom because the Bible is the Word of God, expressed in the words of mankind. It contains the stories of believers' *experiences* of God, and reaches its climax in their de-
scriptions of the liberating effects of Jesus' resurrection from

the dead. As we read the Bible, we are empowered to *know* Jesus from within—and we have God's guarantee that the Spirit of truth will produce freedom (Jn 8:32).

Knowing something "about" Jesus is ineffective because God is not an *idea,* and Christianity is not a *doctrine;* it is a way of life that is enriched by grace, and a way of life in which growth occurs through a deeper and deeper awareness of God's power *from within.* It is in the process of listening attentively to the Word of God that the committed Christian can come to know Jesus personally. People who merely know "about" Jesus are usually content to say "I believe" without realizing that they have not developed a *relationship* that is close enough to produce trust.

The best way to develop and nurture trust in Jesus is to keep reading the Bible. Although it cannot be read like a piece of contemporary literature (because the context in which the scriptures were written in has changed), the footnotes and the introductions to each book in the more recent translations provide enough background information to clarify the basic messages God intends.

The *Old Testament* is largely made up of the law (the ten commandments) and the writings of the prophets who served as God's spokesmen by calling the people to repentance for their sins. Although developing a balanced understanding of the Old and New Testaments is time-consuming, it leads into the mystery and adventure of faith. Just as the Old Testament is fulfilled in the New, the New Testament is hidden in the Old. The exuberance that characterized the liberation of the Israelites from captivity in Egypt was a mere glimpse of the future joy that would flow from the resurrection. A mature response to the Bible as the Word of God always calls for an appreciation of how the Old Testament and the New Testament are complementary.

The *New Testament* is made up primarily of gospels and letters that focus on the teachings and life of Jesus Christ. The more you read both the Old Testament and the New Testament the quicker you will grasp their inter-relationship; as you do, the image of Jesus as God's Word made flesh will become sharper as God plants the seeds of his divine love in your heart. His input is so powerful that it is difficult to study the Bible with an open mind without being touched. The more open you are, and the more childlike your trust, the more powerful God's message will become. Incidentally, the dynamic exchange of messages that results from reading the Bible illustrates why prayer is best understood as a dialogue.

Because Jesus is literally God's Word made flesh, he is the *fullness* of God's revelation; we should expect to spend a lifetime deepening our appreciation of the depth of his love as it is revealed in the pages of sacred scripture. While methods of interpretation may differ, the goal of Christians should be the same: to use the Bible to deepen personal relationships with Jesus. While Protestants tend to emphasize individual interpretation, Roman Catholics rely on a more collective interpretation that is called "tradition." The following excerpt from the documents of the Second Vatican Council explains how the Roman Catholic concept of "tradition" differs from custom.

> The Tradition that comes from the apostles makes progress in the church with the help of the Holy Spirit. There is growth in insight into the realities and words that are being passed on (Dogmatic Constitution on Divine Revelation, #8).

Catholics entrust the process of separating "tradition" from custom to their bishops (who are viewed as teachers and apostolic successors). Scholars, theologians, and the experience and wisdom of the community of believers also provide relevant inputs for their consideration. Because this concept of "tradition" is meant to be "*progress*-ive," it should be characterized by the unique growth that results from the application of the spiritual gifts of wisdom and insight. Authentic tradition always has a forward looking growth-oriented component; in contrast, customs reflect *past* values.

Tradition in the spiritual sense arises out of the complexity of revelation and the necessity of nurturing growth in insight. As the church encounters change in the world, it will either grow as a dynamic living organism, or stagnate. The reflective prayerful application of tradition calls for new approaches and fresh ideas; God's message is not being changed (it cannot be changed by mankind); our understanding of it is being guided by the Holy Spirit. *Tradition is the result of faith applied to the problems we encounter in our daily lives.*

When individual members choose to cling to custom or habit because they fear change, the church loses some of its vitality; the whole body of Christ can be weakened if passivity becomes widespread. Because people who cling to religious customs often use the structure of religion to satisfy an inordinate need for security, they do not want to be taught anything new.

If we are to fulfill our role in the body of Christ, we must allow God's Word and Spirit to teach us and *transform* us from within. By giving us a vocation to proclaim his Word, God not only nurtures our own spiritual growth, he simultaneously provides the world with timely opportunities to encounter the body of Christ. Jesus did not intend to provide us with a spiritual "security blanket"; his goal was to breathe his Spirit into our hearts to enable us to keep announcing the good news of salvation to mankind.

Spiritual life and transformation do not come easy. It is difficult to be transformed because it is difficult to give up control of our lives to anyone, including God. Transformation involves risk and the possibility of rejection—even by people we love. This is what Jesus meant when he said:

> Do not suppose that my mission on earth is to spread peace.
> My mission is to spread, not peace, but division. I have come
> to set a man at odds with his father, a daughter with her
> mother, a daughter-in-law with her mother-in-law . . . (Mt
> 10:34–35).

Balanced and harmonious growth, transformation, and conversion lie at the heart of Christianity. Perhaps this is what
prompted G.K. Chesterton to observe: "It's not that Christianity has been tried and found wanting. It's been found hard and
not tried." "Joining" the church as if it were simply an institution is the equivalent of not trying!

It is impossible to listen to the Word of God without eventually learning to appreciate that the church is nothing less than a
daily *participation* in suffering, death, and resurrection, *with
Jesus, in the body of Christ.* The grace-power and sense of spiritual
direction that active participation in the body of Christ creates is
the subject of the next chapter.

CHAPTER SIX

Are You Experiencing Grace as *Power?*

It is difficult to sit on a two-wheeled bicycle when it is standing still; with a little forward motion it becomes easy. Similarly, maintaining a sense of balance in life is easier if we are "motive-ated" and therefore moving toward the attainment of goals (both spiritual and temporal). Keeping the ever present danger of complacency in mind, let's get started—and let's keep moving!

Years ago, while I was still studying to be a priest, I helped to give a retreat for some teenagers. The room that we used for our conferences had a large piece of butcher block paper on the wall that served as a graffiti board; it contained the following prayer:

Hard to tell you how I feel
everything is so unreal.
Hard to tell you where I've been
everything was so pretend.
When you're born they carry you
when you're dead they bury you.
In between you're on your own
hard to stand there all alone.
Lord this hill is hard to climb;
going to climb it one more time.

Someone's crying down the hall
dying they tell it all.
Lord this life is a hard thing to get through
but yet hard to leave.

Dawn

Dawn had lived through some difficult years, including a stint in
juvenile hall. I don't know whether she wrote this poem, but it
described her well.

What Dawn was crying out for, and what most of us need, is
grace-power, movement toward God, and someone to share the
mystical experience of spiritual life. When we are in a spiritual
relationship with God, we are automatically uplifted and empowered to act with new freedom. The more we grow, the more
our spiritual consciousness rises; as it does, the need for communication with others who have penetrated deeply into the mystery of faith becomes increasingly important. It is only through
communication such as this that the sacrament of matrimony
can truly reflect the unity that exists between Christ and his
people, the church.

When the apostles expressed anxiety over being left alone,
Jesus promised them the gift of his Spirit (Jn 16:4b–16). He
fulfilled that promise at Pentecost, and he continues to fulfill
that promise each day as the Spirit sustains and empowers the
church. This power grows through prayerful communication
with God, becomes stronger through the exercise of faith, and
ultimately reaches its peak in the experience of salvation. Therefore the crippling sense of powerlessness that is often blamed
on large institutions is self-inflicted; we cripple ourselves when-
ever we resist the indwelling of the Holy Spirit.

The grace that the Holy Spirit provides is God's gift of power
and direction. It serves as the fuel that makes the process of our
"conversion" possible and gives us the energy we need to speak

out and act for God. In short, it is what allows God to accomplish great things through us despite our weakness.

> I cannot even understand my own actions. I do not do what I want to do but what I hate. . . . The desire to do right is there but not the power (Rom 7:15, 18b).

Here Paul is setting a contrast between that part of him that is dominated by natural, temporal needs, and that part of him that is being influenced by Jesus Christ. His point is that those who accept Christ and who are filled with his Spirit are empowered with enough freedom to live a new life. This is what it means to say that Jesus has liberated us from slavery to sin and death, and this is what our conversion is all about. Ultimately, our struggle against the forces of evil will be victorious—not because of our merits, but because of the power of God's great love, a love expressed by Jesus' suffering and death, a power manifested by his resurrection, and a power we can share in if we are willing to immerse ourselves in the pain and suffering that is symbolized by the water of baptism.

Those who describe themselves as "religious" may derive good feelings when they attend rituals—without ever being graced or empowered to do anything. These good feelings can become dangerous if they become an obstacle to baptismal promises to be *participants* in Jesus' suffering and death. Despite the pain, the weaker we are, the more powerless we feel, the more dramatic our experience of God's power can be. Christ responded to Paul's prayer for relief (from an unknown affliction) in these words: "My grace is enough for you, for in weakness power reaches perfection" (2 Cor 12:9). Instead of removing it, Christ told him that the weaker he was, the greater the grace-power at his disposal. Weakness increases our potential as witnesses for Christ! This illustrates why ministry is not a vocation for the strongest members of the church, or for a profes-

sional clergy. Each of us has been invited by Christ to be a
follower; therefore each of us has been called to an active ministry. At baptism we were empowered to fulfill a mission (literally "co-missioned") as prophets—to share the kingdom, the
power, and the glory of spiritual life.

This chapter has been concerned with the nature and purpose of God's power. Each scriptural reference focused on the
theme of power to give you an incentive to begin or to renew
your search for truth. May your search soon enrich your life and
help you to live in a communion of power in the church; in
Paul's words, originally written to the church at Ephesus:

> May the God of our Lord Jesus Christ, the Father of glory,
> grant you a spirit of wisdom and insight to know him clearly.
> May he enlighten your innermost vision that you may know
> the great hope to which he has called you, the wealth of his
> glorious heritage to be distributed among the members of the
> church, and the immeasurable scope of his power in us who
> believe (Eph 1:17–19).

Notice that Paul's emphasis is on personal knowledge of Christ,
and on the experience of his presence through the indwelling of
the Holy Spirit. Knowing about God, or about the history of the
church, or knowing its doctrines, dogmas, and laws, is nothing
but a step toward the experience of the power of spirituality.

Now is the time to experience God's power from within, to
become like a conduit through which his power flows. To become "gracious" people we need only apply this power to serve
others. As we prayerfully dialogue with God, we will eventually
begin to discern a purpose, a cause, something that excites us,
something that can help us to integrate our unique talents to
reach the goals that God has planned for us.

The next chapter will deal with the challenge of using the
power of God's grace to deal with the distractions and role-
conflicts imposed by our culture.

CHAPTER SEVEN

What Effect Is Culture Having on Your Responses to God?

The purpose of this chapter is to examine the effects of our culture on spiritual life.

Economic, social and political institutions are exerting an increasingly powerful influence on the quality of human life. Fueled by an insatiable appetite for economic growth, and under the influence of corporations, technology is accelerating the changes we experience without providing adequate safeguards to protect the quality of our lives. For example, smog and toxic wastes are being dumped into the environment by corporations that are unwilling to suffer the competitive disadvantage of paying for safe disposal. Inevitably, someone has to pay for it; too often that "someone" is an innocent victim. Similarly, though fully aware of the danger, corporations have produced automobiles whose gas tanks explode in rear end collisions, and tires whose tread separates at high speed. All this happens because it is mutually advantageous to particular dominant institutions, and because individuals do not know how to protect themselves.

Each institution has a specific interest or motive, and a structure that is uniquely fitted to its own purpose. Profit-seeking corporations are carefully structured to plan, organize, coordinate, and control the attainment of the goal of making money for their stockholders; they do so by manufacturing and selling products. They exist primarily to make a profit; any consideration of the effects of their products on the quality of life is secondary. Corporations are not just servants of the market, or of consumers. Corporations are self-seeking entities that spread their influence through marketing, by lobbying, and by trading favors.

Large organizations raise three dangers. First, the existence of separate economic, social, political, and religious entities (each with its own set of values to promote) tends to create role conflicts for their members; for example, the necessity of keeping a job is sufficiently compelling to discourage employees from speaking out against the organizations that pay their salaries.

The second threat is that as responsibilities become more structured and specialized, "means" such as rules tend to become increasingly more important than "ends" (purposes or goals). This bureaucratic inversion of means and ends results because of the heavy emphasis that is placed on conformity to the tasks and roles. What is important is that the individual worker knows his or her specialty well, and that his or her performance *conforms* to the explicit policies, procedures, and rules. In other words, so much emphasis ends up being placed on conformity that the healthy dreams of potentially creative people are stifled.

In the institutional church (which is a powerful cultural force), bureaupathological behavior causes a significant problem by communicating the importance of conformity to rules instead of allowing the communion that God wants us to share, and the communities that God wants us to build, to speak for themselves. The threat is significant because of the unique means by which the church is meant to proclaim the "good news." The church is unique because it is the body of Christ, and the body (its "medium") is "the message." When the institutional model of the church is dominant, doctrines, dogmas, and laws (that are merely the *means* that provide structure) tend to displace the *ends* of community and communion; willingness to accept institutional dominance compounds the problem.

The third problem is that our culture conditions us to be hungry for "success"; this inclines us to construct an elaborate set of religious beliefs that we can use to measure our "performance." Performance isn't an issue with God—the church's purpose is to be the body of Christ—and to allow *unity* in the body to communicate the "good news" of salvation; it can do so with convincing power. (Chapter 12 will focus on this.) The function of the institutional structure is to help plan, organize, coordinate, and control the bodily process of proclaiming. People will judge the authenticity of its message less by the preciseness of its doctrines, dogmas, and laws, and more by the spiritual bond that unites its members.

The predominance of the institutional model in the minds of many believers is apparent from their tendency to describe church in terms of its hierarchical structure. Even those who implicitly recognize the centrality of witnessing seem content to leave too much of it to "professional" clergy and religious.

The prevalence of institutional dominance in our society has created a crippling sense of powerlessness and apathy, and a convenient rationale for passivity. While TV sets drone on and on, the vicious circle of institutional dominance, powerlessness, apathy, and passivity goes 'round and 'round. But every Christian has been "co-missioned"—by and with Christ—to displace this passivity with actions that build community.

Large institutions can become more benevolent agents of change if we act as stewards of God who have access to divine wisdom and power. Abraham Lincoln once said, "Nearly all men can stand adversity; if you really want to test a man's character, give him power." Our culture is being less adversely affected by institutions than by the "ab-use" of power by its members. Too many people are eager to exercise their temporal power with indulgent self-interest, and too few are able to exercise their spirituality by putting God's grace-power to work. *The best way to respond to God with faith is to use the internal "grace-power" that God offers to his disciples to overcome the anxieties that result from seeking too much pleasure and from accepting too many external signs of success; in doing so, we will stretch ourselves—and therefore our institutions—beyond their apparent limits!*

In short, the prescription that can offset the negative effects of culture is prophetic *action.* The next three chapters will focus on some preliminary decisions that lead up to the most important of all human actions—sustaining a personal relationship with Jesus.

Part Three

Signs of Life

CHAPTER EIGHT

Are You Searching for Truth?

It is easy for any truth to become obscure in our culture, even the truth that reflects the presence of God. The world of advertising is filled with contradictory and often misleading messages that are intended to get us to part with some of our money. "Wear this brand of clothing, and you will be more attractive." "Use this cream, and your wrinkles will disappear." "Smoke these cigarettes, and you will be satisfied." While a brokerage firm urges us to invest our money on one TV channel, a dozen other commercials are simultaneously trying to coax us into spending every penny, and even to borrow at "attractive" rates that far exceed what our savings accounts are earning. The broader our perspective, the more apparent the contradictions become.

While technology continues to develop new and better means of communication, the truth that God communicates has become a rare and precious commodity—not because of its scarce supply, but because too few people are receiving it well enough to share it with others. The truth that God wants us to experience is that his love is *unconditional*, and that instead of trying to earn it, we ought to help him share it.

The purpose of this chapter is to explore the importance of searching for God's truth in a culture that frequently emphasizes superficialities.

When applied to humans, truth in its deepest sense is a mat-

ter of seeing integrity as "wholeness." To fail to appreciate the
depth of God's love is to be neither fully human nor fully alive.
The vacuum that results makes us, and the society in which we
live, vulnerable to a variety of "dis-eases." Thus, much of the
social and emotional distress that characterizes our society is the
result of self-images that are "poor" precisely because they are
incomplete. In contrast, because Dr. Martin Luther King, Jr.
knew God loved him, he was able to withstand taunts and slurs
that went far beyond the proprieties of criticism. His integrity
and inner strength was less a matter of telling the truth than it
was a matter of searching for God's truth, finding it, and
thereby becoming whole or complete. One person with integrity
can make an astonishing difference!

Today's role conflicts present a formidable obstacle to the
achievement of integrity. To allow economic, political, and social institutions to define our identity is to exchange our capacity to reflect the indwelling presence of God for the emptiness
of external symbols such as job titles, power, and money. The
better, more Christian choice is twofold. First, to become a
seeker. And second, to be empowered by the Holy Spirit and
thereby become "gifted" with the wisdom, insight, and courage,
we need to re-form (as prophets) our cultural institutions. Corporations and governments will not have a conscience unless *we*
provide it. In an age characterized by scarce resources, our
ability to work as a team truly dedicated to bringing out the best
in ourselves and in each other can turn failure into success.

If you are not certain that you have decided to seek truth,
apply the test that Jesus gave to Pilate: "The reason why I came
into the world is to testify to the truth. Anyone committed to the
truth hears my voice" (Jn 18:37b). Do you "hear his voice" by
reading the Bible regularly? By studying the Bible to deepen
your personal relationship? By being "involved" with a Christian community? If so, you are searching for truth in the right
places. Saying "yes" is not a one-time decision; neither is it

necessary to search day and night. All that is required is an appreciation of the importance of being a seeker, and a willingness to keep on questioning and evaluating.

The next chapter will focus on the importance of making this search while free from coercion by others.

CHAPTER NINE

Are You Free from External Coercion?

The purpose of this chapter is to examine the effect that *others* have on our willingness to become disciples.

> There were many among the Sanhedrin who believed in him;
> but they refused to admit it because of the Pharisees, for fear
> that they might be ejected from the synagogue. They pre-
> ferred the praise of men to the glory of God (Jn 12:42–43).

In this example, anxiety acted like a cancer that divided the people whom Jesus was trying to unite. The members of the Sanhedrin who wanted to believe in Jesus allowed themselves to be coerced by the Pharisees out of "fear that they might be ejected from the synagogue."

The best thing that others can do for us is to set a good example and help to create an environment in which Jesus arouses our curiosity. Unfortunately, apathy or even opposition is closer to the norm. Paul's letter to the Romans begins with a stern warning that God's wrath will be directed toward anyone who deliberately acts in opposition to spreading the message of truth. "The wrath of God is being revealed from heaven against the irreligious and perverse spirit of men . . . who hinder the truth" (Rom 1:18). Notice that even those who are "just" apathetic are in fact hindering the proclamation of the truth. In the process they are harming themselves and all those who still hunger to hear the good news that it contains.

The best thing we can do for ourselves is to seek out communities that, when faced with problems, seek enlightenment from the Spirit of truth. If we settle for anything less, it may have a devastating effect on our spiritual life. Years ago I met a woman who lived in a parish that was becoming racially integrated. She said that she had left the Roman Catholic Church because her pastor never confronted the tensions that resulted. This should not have been much of a surprise, for it is unlikely that much meaningful dialogue had been exchanged in her parish for years. If we do not take advantage of opportunities to be transformed by the Spirit of truth, we will inevitably cause ourselves and others to suffer.

Ask yourself the following questions to help decide whether you have adequate freedom from external coercion:

> Am I strong enough to share my faith with others even when they are critical?
>
> If it becomes necessary, am I willing to be assertive about pursuing my spiritual needs?
>
> Have I persevered in making a search for truth even when those around me have become apathetic?

If you can say "yes" to the above questions, you probably have enough freedom to proceed. On the other hand, if others are influencing you to concentrate on temporal values, try to appreciate how their external coercion is affecting your ability to choose to love God, neighbor, or self; if necessary, make a commitment to work harder at not allowing anyone to force you into, or away from, a relationship with Jesus. Although you will never be totally free from external coercion in this life, you should be aware of the danger of turning away from the Spirit of truth.

The next chapter will examine freedom from a more internal or psychological perspective.

CHAPTER TEN

Are You Free from Internal Coercion?

This chapter will examine freedom from a more *internal* or psychological perspective; its purpose is to identify choices that may be harmful to our spiritual health. For example, perceptions of God that are framed solely by an intellectual acceptance of religious doctrines, dogmas, and laws, or that are primarily based on feelings, create little incentive for timely and prayerful contemplation. The problem is rooted in our need for security; concepts that have been learned too well and feelings that are too comfortable tend to be repeated even if they have become obstacles to spiritual growth. Thoughtlessly clinging to the past is a common symptom of internal coercion.

Freedom from internal coercion allows us to take better advantage of present opportunities. God wants us to use our freedom to update and review what we have been taught, and to balance the equation that exists between growing on the one side, and thinking, learning, adapting, and prudent risk-taking on the other. This is something most of the scribes and Pharisees were never able to do.

Jesus encountered many people whose vision was so limited by past experience that they were not flexible enough to comprehend what he was saying and doing. He told them stories (parables) that made his message as clear and concise as possible. "I use parables when I speak to them because they look but do not see, they listen but do not hear or understand" (Mt

13:13). Quite often he was referring specifically to the Pharisees who actually prided themselves on their legalism. Because what they had been taught was so comfortable to hold onto, they simply closed their minds to what he was saying and doing. We face the same difficulty; legalistic teaching and learning is potentially dangerous, especially for youngsters. When young people are taught in a stern and dogmatic manner, their lessons often "stick" so well that they may remain unquestioned for a lifetime.

Because communication is a two-way process that involves the giving and receiving of messages, the Pharisees' close-minded rigidity apparently prevented them from recognizing how Jesus was fulfilling the Old Testament prophecies about the messiah. On the bottom line, some were probably guilty of no more than being afraid to make a mistake about teachings that they sincerely regarded as sacred. Seen in this light, the Pharisees become victims of misguided religious zeal. Whatever sins they committed may have resulted from dogmatic teaching methods and their subsequent unwillingness or inability to regain their internal freedom.

In the parable of the sower and the seed, Jesus described those who are able to use their internal freedom to make sound judgments as "good ground." "The seed on good ground are those who hear the word in a spirit of openness, retain it, and bear fruit through perseverance" (Lk 8:15). If we are open to the Word of God, and if we persevere in maintaining a personal relationship with Christ, our liberation from the forces of sin and death is guaranteed, both now and forever. Internal freedom allows us to be open to God, to become "good ground," and to become more sensitive to the value of human life and its potential for growth.

Openness and internal freedom pave the way for "conversion." When Jesus healed a crippled man on the sabbath, he violated Jewish law that prohibited any "work." Some who wit-

nessed the event wanted to use it as an excuse to kill him! Jesus
replied to their murmuring by saying: "Stop judging by appearances and make an honest judgment" (Jn 7:24). Our challenge
is much the same: to use our freedom to search for the meaning
that lies below the surface of our observations, and to make
decisions that generate spiritual growth and renewal.

Be forewarned—openness and internal freedom are costly to
maintain, for the more open we are and the more freedom we
have, the more vulnerable we also become to the pain caused by
rejection and misunderstanding; those who are not equally
open and free may judge us harshly for responding enthusiasti-
cally to a "sower" whom they neither perceive nor understand.
This happened to the Old Testament prophets, who were less
predictors of the future than they were proclaimer's of God's
truth, a truth that was either too painful or too confusing for
others to hear. "No prophet is without honor except in his
native place, indeed in his own house" (Mt 13:57b).

You can test your internal freedom by examining the quality
of your decisions. One of the primary purposes of this book is to
provide you with a framework that isolates the decisions you are
making in response to God.

How well are you responding to God? Are you free? Use
Table 10.1 as a guideline. If your responses to God are based
largely on what you were taught as a child, if obedience is more
important than relationships, if feelings and comfortable rou-
tines are more important than participation in the mystery and
adventure of faith, you may not have enough internal freedom.
Healthy responses to God continuously blend elements that
have been taught, felt, *and thought.*

Think about the following principles before going any further:

1. People tend to resist change, even change for the better.
2. Proclaiming the truth (especially when it conflicts with
   popular beliefs) requires courage.

Table 10.1 *Responding to God*

Response Primarily Based On:	Response Primarily Expressed By:	Focus Is On:	Free?
What's been taught	Obedience	Externals	No
What's felt	Comfortable routines	Feeling secure	No
Thought and reflection	Faith and decisions	Doing and deciding	No
All of the above	All of the above	All of the above	Yes

3. Unquestioned beliefs and stale assumptions can block spiritual growth.
4. People who have closed themselves to change and personal growth and who are complacent tend to honor and support those who share their viewpoints—even if they are illusions.
5. People who confuse illusions with reality do not always welcome those who proclaim the truth.
6. Leadership and popularity are often incompatible.

We are now at a major crossroad. What we have covered thus far has focused on decisions that are preliminary. The next decision (which we will examine in the following chapter) touches the heart of Christianity: it is whether you are making your relationship with Jesus *sufficiently personal.*

CHAPTER ELEVEN

Is Your Relationship with Jesus Sufficiently Personal?

When God attracted Moses to a flaming bush, he called out:

> "Come no nearer! Remove the sandals from your feet, for the place where you stand is holy ground. I am the God of your father," he continued, "the God of Abraham, the God of Isaac, the God of Jacob." Moses hid his face for he was afraid to look at God (Ex 3:5–6).

Moses' initial reaction of reluctance and confusion was predictable; in the Old Testament, God is described as a distant figure who strikes fear in the hearts of the Israelites. Those who communicated with him were fearful enough to keep their distance.

The purpose of this chapter is to examine the significance of a healthy, close relationship with Jesus.

The symbols that the biblical authors used to express the distance between God and mankind included mountains, earthquakes, clouds, lightning, and fire. The setting for the covenant that God made with Moses at Mount Sinai includes them all!

> On the morning of the third day there were peals of thunder and lightning, and a heavy cloud over the mountain. . . . Mount Sinai was all wrapped up in smoke, for the Lord came

down upon it in fire. The smoke rose from it as though from a furnace, and the whole mountain trembled violently (Ex 19:16–18).

Because this imagery was fashioned at an early stage in revelation, it paints only an interim, primitive picture of God.

The anxiety suggested by these symbols continued while the Israelites struggled to live up to the covenant that they made with God through Moses. In exchange for their obedience to the law (the ten commandments), God had promised: ". . . you shall be my special possession, dearer to me than all other people . . ." (Ex 19:5). Their disobedience, which eventually shattered the old covenant, was the reason for the prophets' familiar call to repentance. Throughout the cycle of sin and call to repentance, the Israelites could not sustain the energy they needed to be obedient.

Through the prophets, the Israelites were gradually given a glimpse of a future that was beyond their comprehension. No prophet expressed it more clearly than Jeremiah:

The days are coming, says the Lord, when I will make a new covenant with the house of Israel and the house of Judah. It will not be like the covenant I made with their fathers the day I took them by the hand to lead them forth from the land of Egypt; for they broke my covenant and I had to show myself their master, says the Lord. But this is the covenant which I will make with the house of Israel after those days, says the Lord. I will place my law within them, and write it upon their hearts; I will be their God and they shall be my people (Jer 31:31–33).

Since they perceived the great distance between God and themselves as "normal," they had no reason to expect that God's

Word would become flesh and dwell *among* them, or that God's Holy Spirit would be breathed *into* them.

John the Baptist, the last and greatest of the prophets, pointed to Jesus as the "Lamb of God." Jesus was indeed a sacrificial lamb, reaching out to embrace us with arms that said "I love you," even as he hung on the cross! By becoming man, and breathing his Spirit into his followers, Jesus has fulfilled God's promise to write his law upon our hearts. Now that God has done his part, we have no one but ourselves to blame if we feel "distant," and we have no legitimate excuses for an impersonal response.

God's call to a personal relationship is universal; just as he called other disciples, he is calling you and me. To Matthew, Jesus said, "Follow me" (Lk 5:27b). To Peter and Andrew, he said, "Come after me" (Mt 4:19). His call is persistent, but gentle. He will neither beg us nor force us, and he offers no special privileges in return.

A decision to be in a personal relationship with Jesus always includes two difficult elements. The first is *self-denial.* Jesus said, "If a man wishes to come after me, he must deny his very self, take up his cross, and begin to follow in my footsteps" (Mt 16:24). To deny oneself is simply to admit that without God, failure is inevitable. When we succeed, false humility may prompt us to say, "It was nothing"; in contrast, true humility contains an element of self-denial because it says, "Whatever good I achieve is the result of my cooperation with God."

The second difficult element is that of service; the closest followers of Jesus are those who serve others. They are not necessarily priests or ministers or members of religious orders; they are just servants, people who are willing to accept opportunities to be like the "good Samaritan." (See Lk 10:25–37.)

By their very nature, self-denial and service point toward the cross. The cross has always been a harsh reminder of the destiny of all Christians, and it remains so today. Though science and

technology have brought us through successive waves of change
in search of a better life, the cross is a reminder that pain and
suffering will inevitably afflict everyone. By accepting the pain
and suffering that are contained in the mystery of faith and
symbolized by the water of baptism, we can unite ourselves to
Jesus and one another. As we experience this mystical unity with
Jesus, our pain and suffering takes on new meaning, and therefore becomes easier to bear. It makes a lot more sense to follow
Paul's example of boasting about what God has done for us (on
the cross) than to boast about what we have done for ourselves
(see Gal 6:14, and 1 Cor 1:18). By God's providence, the cross is
the vehicle by which we share in the resurrection of Jesus Christ.
Through the cross we are borne aloft on what songwriter Bobby
Hurd has called, "Wings of Wood."

Harsh as it may seem, the cross that we have been called to
carry as followers of Jesus comes with promises of refreshment
and enlightenment:

> Come to me, all you who are weary and find life burdensome,
> and I will refresh you. Take my yoke upon your shoulders and
> learn from me, for I am gentle and humble of heart. Your
> souls will find rest for my yoke is easy and my burden light (Mt
> 11:28–30).

Compared with the "yoke" of the laws imposed by the Pharisees, Jesus' "yoke" fits well; and because his empowering Spirit
dwells within, our burden is lightened.

Apathy and indifference are clearly a rejection of our invitation to be followers; so too is any form of "neutrality." We must
make a decision. "He who is not with me is against me, and he
who does not gather with me scatters" (Mt 12:30). Neutrality is
a rejection. Procrastination is a rejection. Delay is a rejection.
Being "too busy" is a rejection.

By definition, Christians are people who have given their relationship with Christ top priority. "The reign of God is like a buried treasure that a man found in a field; he hid it again and rejoicing at his find went and sold all he had and bought that field" (Mt 13:44). The emphasis in this parable is on the rejoicing that follows the discovery of something extremely valuable. The man found a treasure that he valued more than all he had; thus he was eager to give up everything to buy it. Likewise, a person who develops a personal relationship with Jesus by reading the scriptures and by fellowshiping with other Christians has also discovered a treasure that is priceless. Anything that he or she must give up as a result has little worth in comparison. The result of a decision to have a personal relationship with Christ is a direct experience of God's indwelling presence.

> Anyone who loves me
> will be true to my word,
> and my Father will live in him;
> we will come to him
> and make our dwelling place with him (Jn 14:23).

In developing a close personal relationship with Jesus, we receive his Spirit, the Spirit of truth.

> The Paraclete, the Holy Spirit
> whom the Father will send in my name,
> will instruct you in everything,
> and remind you of all that I told you (Jn 14:26).

John's account of Pentecost describes the beginning of the church as the moment when Jesus breathes on the apostles and says, "Receive the Holy Spirit" (Jn 20:22). Through the indwelling presence of the Holy Spirit, the church continues to function as the body of Christ to this very day. Serious sins, sins that involve a rejection of Christ and a fundamental break in our personal relationship with him, are literally deadly, or "mortal," because their effect is to strip us of the grace-power that the Holy Spirit provides.

In the Old Testament, sinful tendencies were expressed by chronic infidelity to the ten commandments. Today, the deadliness of sin ranges from apathy to outright hostility to Jesus. Eventually, the result (no wholesome sharing of spiritual life) can become permanently fixed as "hell."

This is an appropriate time to pause and reflect on your relationship with Jesus. Keep in mind that openness is an essential component of effective prayer, and use the material in this and the preceding three chapters to reflect upon the quality of your response. How personal is your relationship with Jesus?

1. Is Jesus a familiar person? Do you know him? (vs. merely knowing "about" him.)
2. Do you dialogue with Jesus? Is your communication two-way? Do you seek spiritual nourishment from God's Word by reading the Bible?
3. Do you experience a sense of mutual attraction? Do you feel compelled to know Jesus better?
4. Do you find yourself desiring to be more like Jesus?
5. Do you experience a personal loss when you endanger your relationship through sin?
6. Are you willing to be God's spokesperson (prophet)?
7. Can you accept God's unconditional love as a *gift* (without asking "Why me?" Without trying to earn it by being "good")?

The more "yes" answers, the deeper your personal relationship.

A decision to have a personal relationship with Jesus is the means by which we literally become part of the body of Christ (the church). The next chapter will explore the effect of healthy personal relationships with Jesus on the church as a whole.

CHAPTER TWELVE

Are You Contributing to the Life of the Church?

Like any living body, the church is a dynamic organism whose individual parts or "members" make unique contributions to the welfare of the whole. The purpose of this chapter is to emphasize the exchange of gifts that takes place in the church, and the synergy that makes the church "dynamic."

In 1 Corinthians 10:17, Paul concludes that by sharing in the eucharistic bread and wine we become, "one body"; this "one body" is equated with the Church in Ephesians 1:23 and Colossians 1:24. The parable of the vine and the branches provides additional insight into the shared life that is characteristic of the dynamic church; the imagery is similar to the Pauline concept of the church as the body of Christ because Christianity is portrayed as a communal way of life in which believers are related to one another as branches are to a life-giving vine.

> I am the vine, you are the branches.
> He who lives in me, and I in him,
> will produce abundantly,
> for apart from me you can do nothing.
> A man who does not live in me
> is like a withered, rejected branch,
> picked up to be thrown into the fire and burnt (Jn 15:5–6).

The "fruitful branches" are the Spirit-actualizing people who are the active "cells" in the body of Christ; as long as they maintain their personal relationship with Jesus, whose Spirit is the only "vine" that can sustain them, they will continue to bear fruit. The lessons of scripture are clear: the Holy Spirit animates the church by providing both the means by which we share in God's divine life, and the spiritual unity that serves to multiply our collective strength.

When the Holy Spirit came upon the disciples on the first Pentecost, they were immediately transformed into bold and effective witnesses. (Read Acts 2:1–4.) The significance of this event is that to this day, Pentecost celebrates the end of the Easter season. Pentecost—the coming of the Holy Spirit—is the event that marks the beginning of a new era in salvation history, the era of the church. Jesus' resurrection began to achieve its purpose (salvation) on the first Pentecost—and it continues to achieve its purpose today as the Holy Spirit empowers the church to witness with the authority of Christ himself.

On the first Pentecost, the apostles were commissioned to proclaim the gospel to all nations, and empowered by the Holy Spirit to be successful. The Holy Spirit offers a similar commission and power to each of us, and the Spirit's lingering power is what makes the church dynamic. Jesus did not form the church as a highly structured organization to contain us. Together with the Father he literally "in-formed" us in his image and likeness in the act of creation, and gave us the freedom to choose to be continuously "transformed" by the power of his Spirit. Then, and now, the essence of life in the Church is more *Spirit*-ual than *organization*-al.

The potential for conflict between a church whose motives are spiritual and a society whose motives are largely temporal should be obvious. Since all large institutions face the danger of inverting means and ends, uniformity (a means) may end up becoming more important than attainment of the spiritual unity that is the church's ultimate goal. And because what is simple tends to expand into what is more complex, the expansion of offices in the church always has the potential to produce a complex structure that overshadows the unifying effects of the Spirit.

To the extent that uniformity suppresses individuality, it acts as an obstacle to the Spirit of truth who wants to em-*power* each of us to make unique contributions—not only for our own welfare, but for the welfare of the whole church. If we exercise our spiritual lives on a part-time basis, or if we allow our lives to become compartmentalized, "religion" becomes just another activity that takes place within guidelines set by a powerful institution. When Christ returns in glory, the integrating power of the Holy Spirit—which we can harness *today*—will no longer be subject to institutional limitations.

The more we allow our individual and collective lives to be unified by the Holy Spirit, the more obvious the church will become as the "sacrament" or sign of Jesus' presence. In *Models of the Church,* Catholic theologian Avery Dulles concluded that the "institutional" model of the church could not stand on its own, but that four other models could. The first of the latter models is the church as "*sacrament.*" Indeed, as the body of Christ, the church is the fundamental sign of Christ's presence in the world. While sacramental rituals are both the signs and the means of personal encounters with Christ, the church itself is the collective sign. Christ empowered the church to fulfill its mission by breathing the unifying power of his Holy Spirit into the disciples; only through collective application of the grace-power that God offers us can the church succeed in the struggle "to reconcile everything in his person . . . making peace through the blood of his cross" (Col 1:20).

Mutual service is one means by which the church is both a sign and an instrument of communion with God and with one another. Thus Christ said: "Anyone among you who aspires to greatness must serve the rest; whoever wants to rank first among you must serve the needs of all" (Mk 10:43b–44). The second model, the Church as *servant,* describes the ministry of those who express their spiritual gifts by continuing the work of Christ among those who are ill, or needy, or blind, and so on. Such service becomes "Christian" because it is motivated by the Spirit of the living God; therefore, its meaning and value transcend what is attainable through "social work."

Because love is both the cause and effect of the church as *communion* (the third of Dulles' models) the church is more than a place where you can "get" baptized or "get" married; likewise, the church is more than a place to go to "receive" communion. The church itself is a communion—a people animated by the Holy Spirit, who are engaged in a process of sharing, encountering, serving, and proclaiming. Because this communion is a spiritual gift, it has an interior quality that speaks for itself through the fellowship that exists in true Christian communities.

These models of church as sacrament, servant, and communion provide three insights into the nature of the dynamic church:

1. The Church as *sacrament* is a sign and instrument of grace.
2. The Church as *servant* nourishes the seeds of love that Christ sows in our hearts.
3. The Church as *communion* exists only through and in our fellowship.

These qualities are meant to be communicated in a prophetical manner. Journals and books are inadequate conveyors of this message; even the best of preachers is handicapped when speaking from a pulpit because communication is best achieved when individuals give of themselves in acts of Christian love. We are God's prophets, and our message is to promote openness to

God, generosity in sharing his gifts, and the blessings associated with spiritual unity.

The church on earth is missionary by nature. Thus Dulles' fourth model is the fundamental one; it is that of being a *herald* to the world. Because communication touches the essence of the church's purpose, this model emphasizes the importance of making the first three models visible. The church fulfills its mission to be "a light to the world" by providing the means by which mankind can see and hear God's truth. Anyone with an open mind who encounters this light can experience his or her own "Passover" as the Spirit of truth liberates from within. Liberation is both the fruit of a healthy spiritual life and the focal point of the church's missionary activities.

The power needed to fulfill the mission of communicating the "good news" is available to all followers of Christ. "You will receive power when the Holy Spirit comes down on you; then you are to be my witnesses in Jerusalem, throughout Judea and Samaria, yes, even to the ends of the earth" (Acts 1:8). This power and this mission are for *all* of us.

Universality of power and mission are the qualities that make a church literally "catholic" (meaning "universal"). Thus, Jesus has instructed *every baptized person:*

> Go into the whole world and proclaim the good news to all creation. The man who believes in it and accepts baptism will be saved; the man who refuses to believe in it will be condemned (Mk 16:15–16).

Because the acceptance of baptism and salvation is a matter of spiritual life and death, God wants all of us to use the power of the Holy Spirit to be his spokespersons—no matter how inadequate we may feel.

Those who are truly open to the Holy Spirit usually cannot resist telling others about their newfound freedom and power.

St. Paul, who was one of the greatest persecutors of the early church, was transformed by just one encounter with the risen Christ:

> Preaching the gospel is not the subject of a boast; I am under compulsion and have no choice. I am ruined if I do not preach it (1 Cor 9:16).

You do not have to be an eloquent speaker to be an effective witness. An articulate person who is not a true disciple of Christ cannot communicate as much as a believer who speaks with conviction. Be convicted! Let your actions speak louder than your words.

We live in a world that is in darkness; the "good news" that God has commissioned us to proclaim is light. God's enlightenment can come only through the church, and the church is us! Jesus said, "You are the light of the world." And, "Your light must shine before men . . ." (Mt 5:14). What we do with our lives, individually and collectively, ought to radiate the presence of Christ. As individuals, our lights flicker because of sin, but together our flickering lights can shine brightly all the time.

Since the purpose of the Church is to proclaim the gospel, and since "the medium is the message," institutional dominance carries with it the danger that bureaupathological behavior will offset the unifying effect of the community's shared belief and experiences. *If that is allowed to happen, what is communicated instead of a dynamic expression of the good news is a centralized hierarchical structure that often suppresses more than it enlightens.* The underlying problem does *not* only stem from what the hierarchy is or is not doing; it also stems from the chronic unwillingness or inability of the laity to play more active roles in the body of Christ. In short, widespread failure on the laity's part to speak prophetically can create an imbalance of power.

Unless everyone shares in the church's prophetic mission, the church, as the body of Christ, is "handicapped." When we were baptized, God commissioned us to nurture spiritual life. Unless we take our prophetical roles seriously, the Church's ability to animate the whole world with the Spirit of Christianity will be diminished. The challenge of being a witness for Christ in the informal groups in which we work and play will never be met if we do not consistently reflect the presence of the Spirit of truth. Because Jesus is the only one who can fill us with his Spirit, deciding to have a personal relationship with him is the key to our effective participation in the dynamic church. Thus the fourth and last insight into the dynamic church has to do with the effect of participation on communication: it is natural for the church to communicate itself! Our desire to share God's good news ought to be instinctive.

> The Church as *herald* communicates itself through the con-
> victions of individual followers as they spontaneously witness
> to Christ in their everyday lives.

To complete this survey of the dynamic church, we must examine the enabling role that authority plays—specifically, how authority functions as power to act. We begin with the premise that all authority and power to act in the church comes from the Holy Spirit. Thus, authority resides not only in a hierarchy, flowing downward from bishops, but also in all the members of the body of Christ—rising from the bottom up! Let's focus on this upward flow. The Holy Spirit graces all members of the church; by his gifts he makes us "fit and ready to undertake various tasks and offices for the renewal and building up of the Church" (*Dogmatic Constitution on the Church*, #12). Therefore, every person who is a baptismal follower of Christ (and therefore a member of the church) is provided by the Holy Spirit with enough "grace-power" to have some measure of authority; by definition, this must include *all* Christians.

When viewed from the bottom up, authority in the church clearly lies both in the community as a whole and in the hierarchy. The degree of authority or power to act will differ according to the particular gifts that the Holy Spirit allocates to each person, and also according to their office, if any. But one thing remains constant: all authority and power is always to be held as a trust for the good of the entire church.

St. Augustine expressed the danger inherent in a "top-down" concentration of authority and power in these words:

> When I am frightened by what I am to you, then I am consoled by what I am with you. To you I am the bishop, with you I am a Christian. The first is an office, the second a grace; the first a danger, the second salvation.

By describing institutional power in terms of an office, and spiritual power in terms of grace and salvation, St. Augustine challenged all those who held offices in the church to pledge themselves to serve others as Christ did. The Second Vatican Council's concept of "collegial" or shared power also supports this notion by pointing out that all bishops are called to work together as servants *for the good of the whole church.*

The complexity of the issues raised by authority in the church will always raise questions regarding institutional abuses and the need for reform. In no way should this be perceived as a threat to the church itself, which is an organic body rather than an institution. As any other "body," the church must reform itself by maintaining natural processes of adaptive growth.

The dynamic church is adaptive by nature because it exists as a manifestation of lives touched by the Spirit of the living God. The gifts that the Spirit releases in individuals continuously effect change through an ongoing process of personal growth and maturity; it is through the adaptive process called "tradition" that the gospel message is made relevant for each succeeding generation.

Institutional reform has actually been constant throughout the history of the church. By the middle ages, the power of the laity was substantially reduced when compared with the early church. In the Catholic Church since Vatican II, the pendulum has begun to shift back toward the center with the recognition that the laity should act on their own initiative.

> The pastors . . . should recognize and promote the dignity and responsibility of the laity in the church. They should willingly use their prudential advice and confidently assign duties to them in the service of the church, leaving them freedom and scope for acting. Indeed, they should give them courage to undertake works on their own initiative. They should with paternal love consider attentively in Christ initial moves, suggestions and desires proposed by the laity (*Dogmatic Constitution on the Church,* #37).

This excerpt describes the character of a "dynamic church" well. Through the power of the Holy Spirit, objectives are shared, vision becomes creative, problems become opportunities, decisions are made at the lowest possible levels, consensus is facilitated, coordination is the by-product of gift-giving, behavior is informal, and risks are willingly taken because they are seen as prerequisites to growth.

Table 12.1 compares the institutional and dynamic models of church. The differences have been emphasized intentionally to dramatize the potential for human growth within the more dynamic models of the church.

The institutional church plays a vital role by providing stability and continuity in the task of proclaiming the gospel message over the centuries. But only the power of the Holy Spirit can foster adaptive growth within the church (both in the commu-

Table 12.1 *Toward a More Balanced Experience of Church*

Institutional Model	Characteristics	Dulles' Four Dynamic Models
handed down	**OBJECTIVES**	greater emphasis on sharing/participation
driven by custom	**VISION**	focused on creativity/innovation
bureaucratically hidden/buried	**PROBLEMS**	opportunities for growth
at higher levels	**DECISION-MAKING**	at lower levels
task-centered: carried out by directive	**COORDINATION**	people-centered: a by-product of the focus on gift-giving
conforming	**BEHAVIOR**	more spontaneous/informal
minimized (to protect)	**RISK**	Maximized (to promote growth)
weaker, less personal	**RELATIONSHIPS**	stronger, more personal

nity and in our individual spiritual lives); this growth-oriented "progress"-ive force is precisely what makes the church dynamic!

Use Table 12.1 to evaluate the quality of your experience. The deeper your relationship with Christ, the more likely you are to develop an awareness of your potential to contribute to the adaptive growth of the church. *Being a "good Catholic" and going "to" church are not as relevant to God as what you are doing to help the church (as the body of Christ) go to the world;* the latter expresses the purpose of the Second Vatican Council.

The next chapter will provide more criteria to help you decide how well you are growing toward full stature, and how well you are contributing to the welfare of the church.

CHAPTER THIRTEEN

Is Your Growth Harmonious and Integral?

The purpose of this chapter is to examine spiritual growth patterns. As we grow toward full stature as beings created in the image and likeness of God, our temporal and religious experiences tend to become more integrated. When we use God's grace to contribute to the life of the church, we are contributing to the completeness of the body of Christ; in effect, we become fully human by becoming part of God's divinity!

The Holy Spirit gives each of us unique gifts—as well as the wisdom and freedom we need to use them as effective stewards. Eventually, we will be held accountable for the harmonious integration of our temporal and spiritual selves as expressed by:

1. the humble receiving and generous giving of gifts
2. the triumph of grace over nature

Our need for balanced growth and active generous sharing of gifts does not come without obstacles. In an age in which specialization has become the norm, too many human lives have become so compartmentalized that the practice of religion is often reduced to participation in rituals that do little more than satisfy our need for security. The church as the body of Christ is meant to be "sacramental" because it alone can become the fundamental sign or symbol of our partnership with Jesus; passive or legalistic expressions of Christianity have no life.

Passivity, boredom, and apathy are symptoms of lives that are both emotionally and spiritually unhealthy. People who are passive often see themselves "victims" of a succession of forces that they may even regard as "hostile"; in actuality, such people are their own worst enemies. In contrast, the health of active Christians is the result of their integrity or "whole"-someness. True integrity is a matter of drawing on the infinite source of power, energy, and enthusiasm provided by the Spirit of truth.

Individually and collectively, self-control in the body of Christ (the church) is better achieved through the indwelling presence of the Holy Spirit than through laws. Consequently, the fullness of Christian life and the perfection of love are possible only through the application of the Spirit's *grace*-power. This unique power plays an essential role in helping us win the inner struggle between good and evil. The struggle begins at birth. Because of "original sin," we are self-centered; baptism is the beginning of a process in which grace triumphs over nature by turning our sinful orientation inside out.

Commitment to ministry is a good sign of the gift-giving and grace that characterize harmonious and integral growth. Therefore, it is the vocation of all Christians, and not just a job for ordained "professionals." Above all, it is an expression of love and a response to our baptismal vocation to share in Christ's ministry as priest, prophet, and king. Keep Jesus' advice in mind: "Give to Caesar what is Caesar's, but give to God what is God's" (Mt 22:21). The best way to give to God what is God's is to use our free will to love others as he did, and to become whole in the process. God does not need our love—but we need to love God, neighbor, and self to achieve inner peace, harmony, and integrity.

The manner in which we spend our time reveals a great deal about the spiritual harmony and integrity in our lives. God

doesn't count the number of hours we spend going to church
meetings or attending services; he simply expects us to reflect
his image *all the time.* This does not mean that we have to get up
on soapboxes and preach on street corners, but it does mean
that people ought to be attracted to Christ as he reveals himself
through us. Until we make an effort to play active roles in the
body of Christ, our growth is neither harmonious nor integral,
and Christ's visibility is somewhat diminished. The challenge we
face is simply to allow our lifestyles let God's peace and joy
speak for themselves.

Because material possessions demand considerable time and
energy, they can become a serious obstacle to harmonious and
integral growth.

> No man can serve two masters. He will either hate one and
> love the other, or be attentive to one and despise the other.
> You cannot give yourself to God and money (Mt 6:24).

According to some scholars, the word "money" in this passage
would be better translated as possessions in general. What Jesus
is saying is that *he* wants to be the center of focus in our lives.

People who are making God their center of focus are mutually attracted to one another. They tend to form small basic
communities that serve as the ideal means by which they can
approach God. As a result, their rituals serve more effectively as
signs of encounter; this is also the subject of the next chapter.
Being an active member of the body of Christ means more than
just going to mass on Sundays, it means following through with
"comm-*union,*" which in turn means sharing enough of yourself
to participate in the social and religious activities that are out-
lined in the typical parish's Sunday bulletin. If you have not
been very active, review Chapters 8 through 13 before going
any further—because commitment and active participation in
the church are prerequisites to fruitful rituals.

The pace of modern life has become so rapid that without realizing it, you may be spending too much time "doing," and too little time "being." If you are committed to baptism, you are one with Christ; and if you are one with Christ, your growth patterns are moving in a harmonious and integral direction. In the next chapter, we will examine the role the sacraments play as *signs* of this harmony and integrity.

CHAPTER FOURTEEN

Is Your Sacramental Life
"Sign-ificant?"

Mankind has used symbols and rituals to respond to God since ancient times. Most Christian symbols are centered on Jesus; through him, the finite and infinite worlds have come together so that they might literally be put in "right order." The purpose of this chapter is to explain how the sacramental signs and symbols that Roman Catholics use serve as expressions of their partnerships with God and neighbor. The seven sacraments are: baptism, confirmation, holy communion, reconciliation, matrimony, holy orders, and anointing of the sick.

In each ritual encounter, Roman Catholics use scripture and tradition to recall how God has acted in salvation history, and then promise to cooperate with him as he continues his plan for the salvation of mankind. The ritual is a fleeting moment:

1. the decisive point where the past, the present, and the future meet
2. the turning point where our commitment to work with God begins to shape the future

The better our understanding of the history of salvation (what God has done for mankind—depicted on the left side of Figure 14.1), the easier it becomes to act out the story of our own

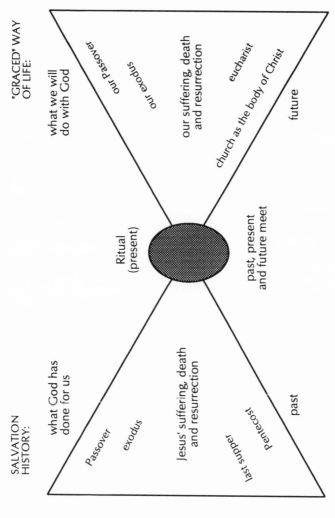

FIGURE 14.1 SACRAMENTS

SALVATION HISTORY:

what God has done for us

Passover

exodus

Jesus' suffering, death and resurrection

last supper

pentecost

past

Ritual (present)

past, present and future meet

"GRACED" WAY OF LIFE:

what we will do with God

our passover

our exodus

our suffering, death and resurrection

church as the body of Christ

eucharist

future

salvation (the "graced" way of life—depicted on the right side of Figure 14.1).

The seven ritual sacraments simultaneously *sign*-ify and cause the grace to flow. If they are to be effective signs, the unity that is the essence of basic Christian communities should be obvious both during—and particularly after—the ritual. Over time, this unity should gradually become more evident as our relationships with God and neighbor are enriched. *Each individual sign of encounter is meant to be extended into daily life to serve as a living proclamation of faith in Jesus Christ;* while each ritual uses an outward sign that is symbolic, it is in our daily lives that the sign value of the sacraments will have their greatest impact on others. Thus we must move beyond the limitations imposed by the classroom model of CCD (as Confraternity of Christian Doctrine) to a more sacramental model of CCD as "Continuing Christian Development"; in this model:

1. all of us are the teachers
2. the "classroom" is daily life
3. and the lessons are taught by the sign value of our sacramental partnerships with God

Table 14.1 summarizes the signs and effects of each sacrament. The enrichment that takes place in each of the above encounters takes place within the context of the network of personal relationships that exist between God and mankind in the church. The enriched human lives that result from our partnership with God are the most effective means that the church has to proclaim the good news of salvation.

Let's look at the individual sacraments, beginning with baptism. The symbolism of the water used in baptism is frequently misunderstood. *Baptism means immersion;* the water is more than a means of cleansing, it is the medium in which we can express a commitment to plunge into the suffering, death, and resurrec-

Table 14.1   *Signs of Encounter with God*

Sacrament	Outward Sign	Result of Our Partnership with God
Baptism	pouring of or *immersion* in water	*dying*—plunging or dipping into the death of Jesus, and *rising*—sharing in his resurrection; reception of the Holy Spirit
Confirmation	imposition of hands and anointing	accepting/strengthening of the gifts of the Holy Spirit
Eucharist	sharing of the Word and the body and blood of Christ	nourishment within the body of Christ
Matrimony	exchange of vows to love unconditionally	a mirror image of Christ's love for the church
Holy Orders	imposition of hands	transmission of Christ's mediating power/authority
Reconciliation	sorrow/contrition	"at-one-ment"
Anointing of the Sick	anointing with oil	strengthening/healing of mind and body

tion of Jesus. An adult who is baptized (or a child who participates through the faith commitment of his or her parents) symbolically dies with Christ as he or she is immersed in the water and rises with Christ as he or she emerges to begin a new (graced) way of life. While the pouring of water is certainly more expedient, it lacks the visual impact of immersion.

In the early church, baptism, *confirmation*, and eucharist (holy communion) were celebrated in one initiation ceremony. Confirmation was later separated, and became the rite of passage into spiritual adulthood. When infant baptism became the norm, confirmation provided young adults with an opportunity to renew the baptismal promises that their parents made for them in infancy.

The intensity of communal life in the early church is described in Acts of the Apostles.

> Those who believed shared all things in common; they would sell their property and goods, dividing everything on the basis of each one's need. They went into the temple area together every day, while in their homes they broke bread. With exultant and sincere hearts they took their meals in common (Acts 2:44–46).

The breaking of bread refers to *holy communion,* which Christ founded while he celebrated Passover (in the appropriate mood of liberation and deliverance) with the disciples. He did so as a means of perpetuating the *new* covenant—which is God's promise to liberate us from captivity to sin and death.

The more conscious we are of the need for liberation—our own "Passover" experience—the more credible our celebration of communion will become to those who are "unchurched." Christ's broken body and blood are a visible expression of God's unconditional love, and those who approach the altar in the manner described in Acts 2:44–46 are simultaneously signifying and causing a bond of fraternal charity with God and one another. Because communion is meant to be both a sign and a cause of unity, the Second Vatican Council described the presence of strangers and silent spectators as "unacceptable" (*Constitution on the Sacred Liturgy,* #47), and called full and active participation by all the people "the primary and indispensable source from which the faithful are to derive the true Christian spirit" (#14). Where there is involvement and fellowship, strangers and spectators become spiritual brothers and sisters.

It is by God's design that we are being called to liberation from within a Christian community. Baptism does wash away the effects of original sin, but not in a magical fashion; when Spirit-filled people work together with Christ as their head, they overcome the effects of their sinful environment by reaching out to serve one another. Each of our sacramental encounters provides a means of achieving unity and peace in love. In *Conjectures of a Guilty Bystander,* Thomas Merton asserts:

> A small, apparently insignificant and disorganized circle of friends united by love and a common venture in Christian witness may be of far greater value to the Church than an apparently thriving organization that is in reality permeated with the frenzies of activistic and ambitious willfulness.

Only in the church and through the power of the Holy Spirit can we hope to live together as spiritual brothers and sisters. One aspect of the mystery of faith is that true communion is possible only at the foot of the cross.

Matrimony, the sacramental name for marriage, provides the community with a sign of Christ's love by requiring the bride and groom to make a public vow to love one another as Christ loves the church. In living out these vows, the couple's vocation is to experience physical, emotional, and spiritual unity.

Because the spiritual dimension of love is often ignored, the "*The Road Less Traveled*" is a clever title for a book on love. M. Scott Peck's concept of love as "the will to nurture spiritual growth" calls for a sacramental partnership between God and mankind in which God provides the "grace" and we provide the will to nurture spiritual growth. The cross that is inevitably on the path that leads to spiritual growth (and the delay of gratification that it stands for) gives matrimony and the other sacraments unique potential as signs of life.

Holy orders is the sacrament that the community uses to signify the transmission of power to the deacons, priests, and bishops who have been chosen to be the principal servants. Their ministry provides the community with yet another sign of God's abiding presence, and gives further expression of the self-sacrificial nature of Christian love.

The sacraments of healing (*reconciliation* or "confession" and the *sacrament of the sick*) provide the spiritual "glue" that keeps our communities together despite the divisive effect of sin. The role of the priest in the sacrament of reconciliation is not to replace God as forgiver, but to provide the sinner with someone who concretely represents the community that has also suffered from the effects of the penitent's specific sins; the priest, as an elder in the community, and on their behalf, receives the sinner's contrition and then pronounces the words of absolution. In the sacrament of the sick, the community gathers with the person who is sick or injured to pray for a spiritual or physical healing.

It is Christ, as the mediator of the new and everlasting covenant, who is the obvious center of focus for all sacramental life. He serves as the object of our worship and the means by which we become temples of his Spirit. As a result of the grace that he provides, life in Christian communities is not restrained, it is enhanced. Whereas "religion" is often regarded as a *constraint,* the presence of the Spirit in Christian communities is the fulfillment of God's promise of *individual and collective liberation.*

Commitment and community are key ingredients in all sacraments. As described above, the commitment is nothing less than a thoughtful and affirmative response to baptism's radical call to an immersion into the suffering and death that Jesus endured on Calvary. And as described above, the effect of baptism is a community formed by the indwelling presence of the Holy Spirit.

The lack of emphasis on community has become a significant problem. To receive a sacrament in isolation or primarily for private gain is to diminish God's purpose and is the equivalent of lighting a lamp and "putting it under a bushel basket" (Mt 5:15). Unfortunately, there are signs of just such darkness:

1. baptisms on Sunday afternoons to avoid "inconveniencing" those at mass
2. marriages and baptisms of those who are, paradoxically, strangers in the parish
3. dwindling numbers of penitents, or repetitious "laundry lists" of sins

The prescription for a cure lies in:

1. understanding that sacraments are not just for our personal gain
2. being willing to use the sacraments in a prophetical manner—as a public expression of a commitment to follow Jesus

Because these are difficult tasks, the next twelve chapters will lay a foundation made up of specific "transformations" that reflect the uniqueness of Christianity. Each of the twelve reflects one aspect of the contrast between salvation and sin/death, or between faith and anxiety, or between prayer and complacency. The first is moving from the acceptance of a fixed ideology to *insight*.

Part Four

Christian Transformations

CHAPTER FIFTEEN

FIXED IDEOLOGY
FIXED IDEOLOGY
FIXED IDEOLOGY
FIXED IDEOLOGY
FIXED IDEOLOGY
FIXED IDEOLOGY
FIXED IDEOLOGY

ACCEPT: FIXED IDEOLOGY?

OR

INSIGHT
INSIGHT
INSIGHT
INSIGHT
INSIGHT
INSIGHT
INSIGHT
INSIGHT
INSIGHT

INSIGHT?

The Advocate, the Holy Spirit that the Father will send in my name—he will teach you everything and remind you of all that I told you (Jn 14:26).

Roman Catholics who are able to grasp the benefits of believing in scripture and tradition benefit from the key role that *insight* plays in spiritual life. Remember, tradition in the spiritual sense is not the same as custom; custom looks toward the past, and tradition faces the future with a hunger for spiritual growth and renewal. Consider this:

1. The Vatican II *Constitution on Divine Revelation places* tradition in the context of "growth in insight into the realities and words that are being passed on" (#8).

2. Prayer is a dialogue that lies on a continuum that begins
    with talking to God—and extends all the way to learning
    how to *think* like God.
3. The difference between the two is *insight!*

Searching for insight is the foundation that supports prayer,
faith, and salvation. Blind acceptance of a fixed ideology may
offer more comfort in the short term, but inevitably produces
even more anxiety. It just doesn't make any sense to respond to
God with anything less than a hunger for insight!

Throughout the centuries, most of the heresies that denied
church dogmas were given names ending in "ism." While certainly not a heresy, "misoneism," hatred or dislike of what is
new or represents change, has created a mentality that causes
some people to block out part or even all of the insights associated with Vatican II reforms. Because the root causes of misoneism in the post-Vatican II church are more psychological
than theological, a new methodology—one that provides a
framework for adaptive change and growth—is more timely
than a new theology. Those who resist change and therefore
judge their own theology as "conservative" would do well to
remind themselves that scripture teaches the truest orthodoxy
of all: "The greatest among you must be your servant" (Mt
23:11).

There are two principal obstacles that tend to make the transition from fixed ideology to insight difficult. The first is that
insight tends to bring the problems associated with being a *servant* into focus, problems that we would rather ignore. When
this temptation arises, remember that the people who get ahead
in life are the ones who would rather solve problems than ignore them, complain about them, or cover them up. The more
problem-solving talent we display in managing our work, the
more successful we will be. Likewise, the more problem-solving
talent we display in managing our spiritual lives, the closer we

come to fulfilling our potential as creatures fashioned in the image and likeness of God.

The second obstacle is that spiritual opportunities make us vulnerable. Here's why: love and morality are calls to share the uniquely personal and powerful gifts that we have received from the Holy Spirit; since they are too big for us to contain, they *must* have an outlet. If that object is blocked for any reason, we suffer.

This pain is not a sign of weakness from either a spiritual or a psychological point of view. From a spiritual point we gain insight into the anguish that Jesus must have felt on the cross. From a psychological point of view, we can take our clue from psychologist Abraham Maslow's hierarchy of motives. For Maslow, the highest human motive is for "self-actualization." In *Motivation and Personality* he asserts that self-actualizing people "customarily have some mission in life, some task to fulfill, some problem outside themselves which enlists much of their energies"; it is significant to note that this mission involves serving others. The spiritually healthiest among us are enlightened enough to *choose* the vulnerability that is linked to serving others! It's the pain of redemption, and the premier sign of a healthy spiritual life.

A Christian's willingness to become vulnerable has unique sign value because it mirrors the depth of *God's* love.

> Though he was in the form of God,
> > he did not deem equality with God
> > something to be grasped at.
> Rather, he emptied himself
> > and took the form of a slave,
> > being born in the likeness of men.
> He was known to be of human estate,
> > and it was thus that he humbled himself,
> > obediently accepting even death,
> > death on a cross (Phil 2:6–8).

The outpouring of love that occurred on Calvary still serves as the model for our call to greatness. Self-sacrificial love conforms us to the image and likeness of God, and helps us to become a source of enlightenment.

Vulnerability is the "stuff" that Christian perfection is made up of. The rich young man whom Jesus encountered (see Mk 10:21) tried to avoid it by keeping his possessions instead of becoming a disciple. If he had taken the opposite path and sacrificed himself for the good of others, grace would have triumphed over nature. From a supernatural perspective, it is in possessing that we actually become vulnerable, and it is in the act of giving that we become graciously and truly free!

People who accept opportunities may become more vulnerable, but they are also "on the move." In the Air Force we called them "fast burners"; in IBM we referred to them as being on the "fast track." This anonymous story captures their sense of motion:

> A young man asked a prominent businessman the secret of his success. He replied, "Be on the alert for little things, and jump at opportunities." "But how can I tell the opportunities when they come?" "You can't," he said. "You just have to keep jumping."

Are you the type of person who seeks the insight and enlightenment that flow from Jesus' teachings? Are you learning to accept salvation as a *gift*, or would you prefer to be given a list of rules to follow? Are you an active member of the church, or do you just attend rituals? Do you participate in Bible studies to deepen your insight into the mystery of our faith?

The scribes and Pharisees provide a good example of the inverse relationship between the acceptance of opportunities to grow spiritually and dogmatic teaching; their teachings created a fixed ideology that prevented them from giving much serious thought to what Jesus was saying and doing in their midst—even though he was fulfilling the prophecies of the messiah they were waiting for! On one occasion, they seized an opportunity for rejection when they noticed Jesus eating with the disciples.

"Why do your disciples not follow the tradition of our ances-tors, but instead take food without purifying their hands?" He said to them, "How accurately Isaiah prophesied about you hypocrites. . . . You disregard God's commandment and cling to what is human tradition" (Mk 7:5–8).

The scribes and Pharisees were well versed in Jewish law, and they were proud of their interpretation and observance of it. Jesus' strong reaction to their behavior provides us with plenty of food for thought.

What Jesus called "human tradition" were the type of cus-toms and habits that frequently result from dogmatic teaching. Customs reflect patterns of habitual activity and are generally passed on from one generation to another. They are not the same as what the Roman Catholic Church calls "tradition," which refers specifically to the authority of the church to inter-pret the Bible for each succeeding generation. This authority, which ultimately rests with Christ, has been entrusted to the apostles and their successors and is directed toward "growth in insight."

The danger of clinging to a fixed ideology (an unchanging set of doctrines, dogmas, and laws) is that we will give too much weight to custom, and not enough weight to the fresh inputs being provided by the Word of God. Jesus is God's Word made flesh—and unless we read God's Word (the Bible), it becomes difficult to relate to him in a personal manner. What we have learned is best treated as a stepping stone in an ongoing process of spiritual renewal and personal growth. What we have learned should be updated and evaluated constantly.

God wants us to use his Word (the Bible) to establish a means of daily dialogue. Jesus did not teach "students" about customs; neither did he die on the cross to establish religious rituals that would allow his followers to *feel* good. Instead, his actions gave them food for thought as he gradually drew them as disciples *into* the mystery and adventure of faith. When we read the Bible, the Holy Spirit will draw us into this timeless mystery—a true adventure that challenges us to keep updating and evaluating the validity of what we have been taught and what we are feeling.

Jesus often used parables to test taught and felt viewpoints, and to stretch minds. "I use parables when I speak to them because they look but do not see, they listen but do not hear or understand" (Mt 13:13). Because the old covenant was incompatible with the new, Jesus said, "Nobody sews a piece of unshrunken cloth on an old cloak" (Mt 9:16). When the patched garment was washed, the unshrunken material would pull the stitches. Unless you make a regular effort to deepen your understanding of who God is, and unless you are growing in insight into the meaning and purpose of the church's doctrines, dogmas, and laws, your beliefs may become as useless as a patch made up of unshrunken cloth.

Charles Kettering's definition of an inventor as "an engineer who doesn't take his education too seriously" should serve as a reminder that we cannot afford to rest on what we have learned in the past. Because the Bible is filled with stories about growth in insight, we can be certain that God wants us to use the gifts of the Holy Spirit to become spiritual inventors. What he wants us to invent is whatever it takes to capitalize on opportunities to grow spiritually; what he wants us to avoid are teachings and feelings that have outlived their usefulness.

Table 15.1 summarizes this chapter by listing some of the characteristics that distinguish insight from a fixed ideology.

Table 15.1

From: Fixed Ideology	To: Insight
Stationary	Dynamic
Protects	Renews
Almost everything I know about God, I learned in CCD (or Catholic school).	I am benefiting from the ongoing exchange that takes place during adult education/Bible studies.
I don't like "the changes."	I am asking enough questions about the changes to internalize their meaning.
"Fundamentalism" (the Bible means *exactly* what it says.	God keeps helping the church to grow in insight/understanding of what the Bible means.
Prayer is mostly "talking" to God.	Prayer includes trying to discern *God's* will.
Faith is mostly "believing" in God.	Faith helps me submit to God's will.
Attending only Latin or "Tridentine" masses.	Appreciating the Vatican II emphasis on active participation at mass
Going to mass every Sunday is enough; I don't have time to get "involved."	I can't participate in the mystery of faith unless I experience relationships & community.
I believe in God.	I want to deepen my relationship with Jesus.
"I don't get much out of _____ ." (mass, confession, *etc.*)	Unless I participate in the mystery of faith, I won't experience the *power* of grace.

CHAPTER SIXTEEN

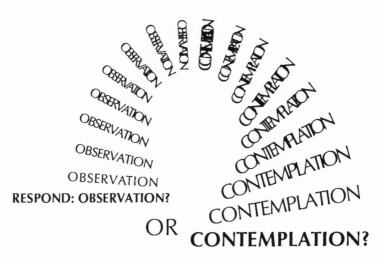

RESPOND: OBSERVATION?

OR **CONTEMPLATION?**

Do not conform yourself to this age but be transformed by the renewal of your mind, that you may discern what is the will of God, what is good, pleasing, and perfect (Rom 12:2).

Fixed ideologies lead toward observation, and insight leads toward the topic of this chapter, contemplation. The benefits of contemplation are twofold:

1. contemplation helps us to get in touch with God's will
2. contemplation helps us to keep what God considers "good, pleasing, and perfect" in sharp focus

The third chapter of the gospel of John tells the story of Nicodemus who, after reflecting on what Jesus was saying and doing, was confused enough to approach him directly. His thoughts must have raised some significant issues because he did so in the secrecy of night (to avoid criticism from the members of the Sanhedrin who were agitated by Jesus' success). As was often the case, Jesus answered one question with another, and *Nicodemus was given even more to think about.*

Because our ability to reason distinguishes us from the rest of creation, we cannot grow to full stature without thinking. As we think about what God reveals through scripture and tradition, we gain a sense of purpose that sheds divine light on the meaning of human life. In *The New Man* Thomas Merton asserts:

> For a man to be alive, he must exercise not only the acts that belong to vegetative and animal life. . . . He must carry on the activities proper to his own specifically human life. He must, that is to say, think intelligently. And above all he must direct his actions by free decisions, made in the light of his own thinking. These decisions, moreover, must tend to his own intellectual and moral and spiritual growth. They must tend to make him more aware of his capacities for knowledge and for free action. They must expand and extend his power to love others, and to dedicate himself to their good: for it is in this act that he finds his own fulfillment.

Life's most important thoughts are those that facilitate love. The consequences of our reflective power are humbling: we are most human when we love, and *when we choose to love as Jesus did, we can begin to appreciate that we resemble God.*

Our ability to reflect is so fundamental to our nature that it stirs our soul; it not only mirrors our resemblance to God, it serves as the basis of our capacity to serve as prophets. Merton says further in *The New Man:*

Man resembles God in as far as he is a contemplative. This
means that man is not only preeminently a thinker, but a
"seer," a prophet who gazes into the deep things of God and
gives utterance to what he sees. He is a man of prayer, a man
of the spirit. And this characteristic is found . . . in the very
structure of man's soul.

Contemplation is to our soul what melody is to our ears, and its
music is the conversion Paul had in mind when he wrote to the
church at Ephesus:

Lay aside your former way of life and the old self which deteri-
orates through illusion and desire, and acquire a fresh spiritual way of thinking. You must put on that new man created
in God's image, whose justice and holiness are born of truth
(Eph 4:22–24).

As we collectively acquire and use this "fresh spiritual way of
thinking" and become "that new man created in God's image,"
we are thrust into the unique experience of truth that is found
only in the body of Christ.

   Think! Look beyond your limits. Draw out the understanding
that lies in your subconscious mind. Time spent in reflective
thought will yield rich dividends; thoughts influence feelings,
and feelings influence behavior. Set aside time to study the Bible, to attend an occasional retreat, and to participate in religious education programs. Time spent in prayerful communities such as Marriage Encounter, Cursillo, or charismatic prayer
groups, and time spent reading books and magazines that focus
on practical applications of God's grace-power, will help you to
keep moving in the right direction.

   Contemplation is not an end in itself; its purpose is to help us
discern God's call to ministry. As Merton says in *Conjectures of a
Guilty Bystander:*

> To take life thoughtlessly, passively as it comes, is to renounce the struggle and purification which are necessary. One cannot simply open his eyes and *see*.

Because the difficulties associated with ministry are an integral part of the process of redemption, there are no acceptable substitutes. Indeed, clinging to a fixed religious ideology to avoid the pain of living out baptismal promises is to walk down a path that leads to even more suffering—because it leads away from God. (See Figure 1.1.)

Because we tend to favor measures of sanctity that are comfortable and relatively painless instead of plunging more deeply into the mystery and adventure of faith, observation cannot serve as a meaningful goal. Once a person decides what makes a "good Catholic," he or she gains a license to live a lifetime without ever having to confront the painful issues that lie on the path that leads toward spiritual growth and renewal, the path Scott Peck so aptly described as "the road less travelled."

The "laundry lists" that many people bring to the sacrament of reconciliation frequently reveal an overemphasis on observation. One example is the spouse whose language and demeanor are filled with symptoms of anger, impatience, and escapist behaviors, but who is offended when I probe beneath the surface and uncover deep-seated marital wounds that have festered into hopelessness. It hardly seems significant to confess "anger" in a marriage that has become spiritually lifeless; yet those whose awareness is monotonously shaped by the limitations of a fixed ideology keep confessing the same sins because they are not contemplating enough to be enlightened and empowered by God's healing word. A more common example of excessive emphasis on observation is the large numbers of penitents who confess missing mass on Sunday—even if there was absolutely no *intention* to do so. Most would rather confess it rather than make the effort first to develop, and then to live with the consequences of, a mature and "informed" conscience.

There is a huge gap between those who choose the path of observation and those who choose the path of contemplation. The Vatican II *Declaration on Religious Liberty* states that we have "a moral obligation to seek the truth, especially religious truth" (#2). This obligatory search for God's truth has no end; if your religious education ended in high school, and if your faith is based on scrupulously observing the CCD lessons that you learned as a child, you may have become dangerously complacent.

Table 16.1 summarizes this chapter by listing some of the characteristics that distinguish contemplation from observation.

Table 16.1

From: Observation	To: Contemplation
Legalism (e.g., "What do I *have* to do to get to heaven?)	What *should* I do to become more Christlike?
Emphasizes "law and order" and discipline: —these are mortal sins —these are venial sins —bringing a written list of sins to confession	Emphasis is on: —thinking —internalizing —understanding —discovering —choosing
Sin is a forbidden *action.*	Sin damages my *relationship* with God.
Doing what I'm told	Being/becoming all that I can be.
Passive	Active
Constrains	Fulfills
Scrupulous	Serene

CHAPTER SEVENTEEN

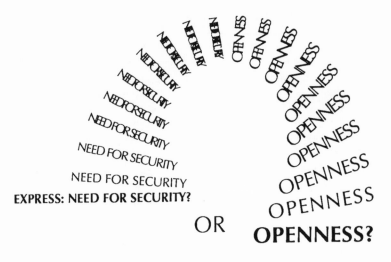

EXPRESS: NEED FOR SECURITY?

OR **OPENNESS?**

After six days Jesus took Peter, James, and John his brother, and led them up a high mountain by themselves. And he was transfigured before them: his face shone like the sun and his clothes became white as light (Mt 17:1–2).

Openness is to contemplation what climate is to plant life. Certain climates are so harsh that plant life is minimal; other climates are so beneficial that they create jungles of growth. Similarly, when we displace our need for security with openness to God, our potential for spiritual growth becomes boundless.

The context for Matthew's account of the transfiguration of Jesus suggests that it was intended to help the disciples to become more open to the meaning of the unpleasant events that were about to occur. The context is twofold:

1. the first prediction of the passion: "Jesus began to show his disciples that he must go to Jerusalem and suffer greatly. . . ." (Mt 16:21)
2. the conditions of discipleship: "Whoever wishes to come after me must deny himself, take up his cross, and follow me." (Mt 16:24)

Peter's impulsive reaction to the former characterized their misunderstanding: "God forbid, Lord!" (Mt 16:22).

Jesus revealed his transfigured image to allow the disciples to have a glimpse of the glory that was their destiny. As baptized Christians, we have been given a preview of that glory too, to equip us with enough energy and hope to persevere in fulfilling our baptismal promises. Relatively few people deliberately and totally close their minds to God; the greater temptation for most of us is either to procrastinate, *or to close our minds because our need for security causes us to reject the pain associated with growth and renewal.* To the extent that we are closed-minded, the communion that should characterize the church as the body of Christ tends to become obscure, if not invisible; if this happens, our sacramental celebrations cannot signify the unity that they should.

Spiritual growth is a by-product of our willingness to allow God to continue to reveal his glory through scripture and tradition. The documents of Vatican II place tradition in the context of "growth in insight" and speak of the scriptures being "more thoroughly understood and constantly actualized in the church" (see *Constitution on Divine Revelation*, #8). This growth and actualization is contingent on a lifetime of openness to God.

The parable of the sower and the seed (Lk 8:4–15) teaches that openness must be combined with patient endurance. "The seed on good ground are those who hear the word in a spirit of openness, retain it, and bear fruit through perseverance." Long-lasting, childlike openness and curiosity can help us to keep growing spiritually long after religious education customarily ceases. The ready acceptance of first-rate adult education programs would seem to indicate that Roman Catholics are hungry for this type of growth.

Prayerful openness to God not only stimulates growth, it helps offset our predilection toward poor self-images by promoting a more generous exchange of gifts. "The things we need come only to us as gifts, and in order to receive them as gifts we have to be open," asserts Merton in *Conjectures of a Guilty Bystander.* By God's design, the church as the body of Christ, provides a unique medium of exchange. Sin is division, and division is sin; when the church or one of its individual members is divided by sin, gifts are not exchanged very well, and the whole body of Christ begins to lose some of its precious vitality.

When our need for security is not tempered by grace, we try to fill the vacuum with activities that make us feel good, or by experiencing the pride associated with fulfilling obligations. Consider the example of the Pharisees. As they observed Jesus eating with tax collectors, they asked:

> "Why does he eat with such as these?" Overhearing the remark, Jesus said to them, "People who are healthy do not need a doctor; sick people do. I have come to call sinners, not the self-righteous" (Mk 2:16–17).

As experts in the law, the Pharisees allowed their intellectual pride to close their minds to God. *We are constantly faced with similar temptations.*

When Jesus made a gift of healing to the man with a crippled hand, he observed the Pharisees waiting for him to violate the sabbath by performing what their closed minds perceived as "unnecessary" work.

> He said to them: "Is it permitted to do a good deed on the
> sabbath—or an evil one? To preserve life—or to destroy it?"
> At this they remained silent. He looked around at them with
> anger, for he was deeply grieved that they had closed their
> minds against him (Mk 3:4–5).

Notice the depth of Jesus' feelings; he felt "anger" and was
"deeply grieved." Anger is not always sinful! And morality is
much more than a set of norms that place constraints on your
behavior; it's a call to be responsive to God and neighbor with a
love that is expressed by an open and free exchange of gifts.

The Pharisees lacked the three key elements of openness:
strength, courage, and compassion. It takes *strength* and *courage*
to be open to God because of the risks associated with unconditional love. And it takes *compassion* to be open to the needy Jesus
in others, to enter into their suffering and misfortune, and, if
possible, to help remove its cause.

Are you "open"? Or are you allowing your need for security
to close your mind? Don't be misled by the cliché "you can't
teach an old dog new tricks." Some of the most open people I
know are retired, and some of the most closed-minded people I
know haven't been out of school very long.

Embracing the cross involves risks that neurotic or anxious
people are reluctant to take. Since most of us are tinged with
some neurosis, we need God's help. Ironically, the quickest way
to become insecure is to pay too much attention to the temporal
needs that tend to consume most of our time and energy. Remember what Jesus said:

> Look at the birds in the sky. They do not sow or reap, they
> gather nothing into barns; yet your heavenly Father feeds
> them. Are you not more important than they? Which of you
> by worrying can add a moment to his life-span? (Mt 6:26–27).

The birds are not passive; they work to build their nests and to seek their food. When we have done the same, the best thing we can do is trust God.

If you are making security an *object* and would rather obey rules and laws than endure the painful *process* of embracing the cross, don't be discouraged. Even the apostles were slow to grasp the meaning and purpose of Jesus' suffering, death, and resurrection. Read and reflect on the meaning of John 20:19–29. When Jesus appeared to the apostles after the resurrection, he had to do three things for them. First, he said: "Peace be with you." Second, he showed them the wounds in his side and the nail marks on his hands. And, third, he breathed on them and said: "Receive the Holy Spirit." Unexpected suffering may knock Spirit-filled Christians off balance, or even off their feet, but the power of the Holy Spirit will eventually restore a spiritual sense of direction. And that direction, even though it leads through suffering and death, also leads directly to the glory of the resurrection!

Because life is difficult, the most insightful road to travel leads through successive cycles of change, self-renewal and adaptive growth. For the Christian, security comes not from the avoidance of the pain and suffering that these cycles bring, but from prayerful acceptance of their baptismal meaning and purpose. Openness is the essence of prayer because it allows contemplation to bear fruit, and because it raises the questions that lead us to deeper levels of the mystery and adventure of faith. *The cycle made up of insight, contemplation, openness, and questions transforms life itself into an unceasing prayer.*

Table 17.1 summarizes this chapter by listing some of the characteristics that distinguish openness from a need for security.

Table 17.1

From: Need for Security	To: Openness
Neurosis/I can't take the risk.	The excitement of mystery and adventure
Clinging	Becoming vulnerable
Resist change	Think, change, grow
Passivity	Activity
Anxiety	Trust (abandonment to the will of God)
Defensiveness	Confident assurance
Feelings of inadequacy	I can do it!
Fear of making mistakes	If it doesn't work out, I'll try again.
It's not worth trying.	I ought to take prudent risks.
Hide	Reveal
Protect	Empower
Reject	Accept
Weakness	Strength/courage

CHAPTER EIGHTEEN

SEEK: "THE ANSWER"?
"THE ANSWER"
"THE ANSWER"
"THE ANSWER"
"THE ANSWER"
"THE ANSWER"
"THE ANSWER"
"THE ANSWER"
"THE ANSWER"

OR

QUESTIONS?
QUESTIONS
QUESTIONS
QUESTIONS
QUESTIONS
QUESTIONS
QUESTIONS
QUESTIONS
QUESTIONS

Why did I not perish at birth,
come forth from the womb and expire? (Job 3:11).

Questions serve two fundamental purposes in a prayerful dialogue with God:

1. they serve as a link between openness and insight
2. they serve as the foundation for a search for life's meaning

In general, questions play the same role in prayer that they do in any dialogue, that of providing "feedback." Feedback is essential because we often attach different meanings to the same words. For example, a tourist in Madrid, Spain who makes plans to meet a native for an "early" dinner may be in for a long wait—restaurants there don't open for dinner until 9:00 p.m. Confusion is almost inevitable in communication that does not provide for questioning and feedback; if you have tried to follow the "simple" instructions that are included with unassembled products, you have probably experienced it.

Job's willingness to ask questions about the reasons for his suffering provides a good example of what a prayerful dialogue with God can do. Job, who knew he was innocent, had to endure the lack of compassion that his friends exhibited when they repeated the commonly held belief that misfortune was punishment for sin and God's invitation to repentance. Instead of settling for a religious answer, "the answer," Job asked God for a meaningful explanation. God's response was:

> Gird up your loins now, like a man;
> I will question you, and you tell me the answers!
> Where were you when I founded the earth?
> Tell me if you have understanding (Job 38:3-4).

Eventually, Job got the point, and responded:

> I know that you can do all things,
> and that no purpose of yours can be hindered.
> I have dealt with great things that I do not understand;
> things too wonderful for me, which I cannot know.
> I had heard of you by word of mouth,
> but now my eye has seen you.
> Therefore I disown what I have said,
> and repent in dust and ashes (Job 42:2-6).

Unless we are willing to enter into similar dialogues with God, we run the risk of drifting through life aimlessly. Because Jesus embodies the mystery of faith, acceptance of his invitation to "come, follow me" leads down unexpected and unknown paths; this is what makes faith an *adventure*. Feedback is critical if we are to establish and then maintain a relationship that is close enough to keep us headed in the right (most meaningful) direction.

Although some religious learning inevitably takes place in classroom settings, it is only through the ongoing process of relating to God in daily life—the way Job did—that we can keep growing to full stature. As our search for questions leads to insight, we also grow as individual cells within the body of Christ. Because the Bible describes a wide variety of healthy responses to God's revelation, we can use it to evaluate the patterns that our own responses are taking.

Jesus frequently raised stimulating questions. When the Pharisees tried to trap him by asking for his opinion about using the Mosaic law to stone an adulterous woman, he turned their attention inward by saying: "Let the man among you who has no sin be the first to cast a stone at her" (Jn 8:7b). Each time he inspires us to question ourselves, he is simultaneously challenging us to become more like him.

Answering God's questions and being willing to face the unknown always involves risk. Skiing provides a good analogy. On a physical level, I can ski all day long without falling, but the more I push myself toward the limits of my ability, the more likely I am to end up in the snow. My success as a skier is better measured by how close I come to skiing as well as I can than by the number of times I fall. Similarly, in the spiritual realm, my success as a Christian is better measured by how well I am using the power of God's grace to ask the risky questions that lead to personal growth than by how many religious rules I choose to follow, or how many rules I have broken in the past.

Here are three simple criteria to help you judge how well you have learned to ask prayerful questions.

1. People who ask adequate questions are able to spend time in solitude. They use the time to evaluate the quality of their lives, to look for opportunities that might otherwise go unnoticed, to think about their goals, and to muster the courage they need to enter more deeply into the mystery of faith.

2. People who ask adequate questions keep growing in their spiritual life. Like inventors, whose fame is attributed to their creative ability to apply science and technology to *things,* saints became famous by applying God's creative grace to *human relationships.* The infinite treasures hidden within the mystery of faith offer opportunities for discovery and adventure that far transcend the limitations of our temporal world; but the paths that lead to them are "less travelled" because they are submerged in the painful waters of baptism.

3. People who ask adequate questions have a goal, and an inclination to act. The causes that excite them may vary, but the results are the same: their actions help to proclaim the good news of salvation, and help to build up the body of Christ.

By persevering in our questioning, we can overcome the limitations of our fallen natures. As we keep our eyes fixed on Jesus, the pain and suffering that we inevitably face can take on a deep meaning and purpose. Death is the "finish line," and the prize that awaits us is "heaven."

Good questions are refreshing. Years ago I spent an hour answering questions from a group of parishioners about my experience of priesthood. The questions were refreshingly candid and stimulating, and they covered a wide variety of topics. I thoroughly enjoyed the interaction. What made this dialogue extraordinary is that the parishioners were all *fifth graders* at the local parish school.

Children ask good questions because they are still curious about the world that surrounds them. Their experience is limited, but they are not too proud to admit it. I'm not sure whether they ask so many questions because they have not yet found "the" answer, or whether they have not yet found "the" answer because they keep asking questions.

Human life is made up of a long chain of unknown experiences that can raise many questions. If we settle for *having* "the" answer, we are likely to stray from the paths that lead to new and unexplored territory; if we focus on *finding* "the" answer, we limit our vision. In either case, both our spiritual and our temporal growth will be stunted until we are more open.

The problems we face often raise questions and opportunities that can draw us into the mystery and adventure of faith. While mysteries are entertaining when they are presented on the pages of a novel or on the narrow horizons of a TV or movie screen (because we will be told "who done it"), they are frustrating in daily life because *we* are responsible for the outcome.

Our inclination to search for "the" answer instead of asking questions arises out of the basic nature of our need for security. This need is so compelling that we may be abusing the freedom of choice that God gave us without even realizing it. Having "the" answer is also compelling because of pride. In school most of us were conditioned to write down the answers for our homework, and to repeat memorized answers on our exams. To this very day, many of us find it difficult to admit that we don't have an answer for every problem. Ironically, fictional problem-solving is becoming recreational, while spiritual problem-solving, which literally has the power to "re-create" us, is frequently ignored. Fictional "mysteries" are now being written in an entirely new genre on "floppy disks." When placed in a personal computer, they allow the user to question witnesses and to search for clues. Sometimes there is even more than one correct solution to the mystery. The object of the game is to enjoy the challenge and to exercise analytical skills. Admittedly, life's problems are too complex to be the subject of a game, but if we simply break them down into parts, they do become easier to solve.

One danger of settling for "the" answer to a complex problem is that it is deceptively easy to find the right answer—*to the wrong problem.* This happens more often than you may think. As a youngster I suffered from frequent sore throats. I followed the usual remedy of "taking two aspirins, drinking a lot of fluids, and calling in the morning." I also took the antibiotics prescribed when the sore throats persisted—which they often did. I was in my thirties by the time a discerning physician suggested that my sore throats might be the result of an allergy. He referred me to a specialist, who confirmed his diagnosis. Once I removed the substance to which I am allergic from my diet, the sore throats came to an abrupt halt. The other doctors had prescribed the right answers (fluids, or rest, or antibiotics, etc.) to the wrong problem (an allergy).

By now it should be apparent that God did not create the church to provide complacent people with a shelter from life's problems. Instead, he breathed his Spirit of truth into the apostles and commissioned them to live a shared life. Their mission was to solve the problems related to original sin *together*—and in the process to make the good news of salvation apparent to mankind! Our growth as Christians is not the result of joining or attending a church; it is the result of our willingness to keep asking the type of questions that lead to God's kingdom.

Every day you will come face to face with opportunities that raise new questions. Don't block them out by settling for "the" answer. Don't just follow all the rules that you were taught. Don't simply attend rituals without understanding what the symbolic actions mean. And if you have difficulty accepting the changes that are taking place in the church, face them creatively as an opportunity to grow. Don't be afraid to ask who? when?

why? how? where? etc. Try to appreciate why the church, as the body of Christ, uses questions that promote change and renewal as a sign of life.

Table 18.1 summarizes this chapter by listing some of the characteristics that distinguish questions from "the answer."

Table 18.1

From: "The" Answer	To: Questions
TA "Parent" language	TA "Adult" language:
—never	—who?
—always	—why?
—shouldn't	—what?
—don't	—where?
	—when?
	—how?
Prejudice	Acceptance
Stereotypes	Respect/appreciation
Fundamentalism (the Bible means *exactly* what it says)	What does this Bible passage mean today? (Interpretation leads to growth in insight)
Security	Risk
Uniformity is more important than unity	Unity and diversity coexist
There's only one way.	Is there a better way?
If God really loved me, he wouldn't let me suffer.	How is my suffering related to the suffering of Jesus?
I can't change.	Adult education programs help me grow.
That's what I was taught.	I'm still learning.

CHAPTER NINETEEN

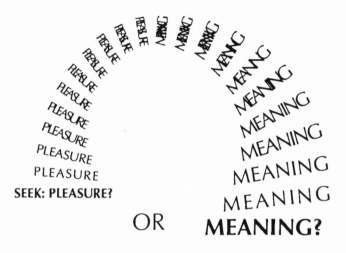

SEEK: PLEASURE?

OR MEANING?

He became angry, and when he refused to enter the house, his father came out and pleaded with him. He said to his father in reply, "Look, all these years I served you and not once did I disobey your orders; yet you never gave me even a young goat to feast on. . . . But when your son returns . . . for him you slaughter the fatted calf?" (Lk 15:28–30).

Unless you ask questions, it is easy to react to the meaning of the parable of "the prodigal son" by feeling superior to the young man who made a fool of himself. To do so is to miss an important part of the message that Luke is trying to convey. *By the end of the parable it is the older brother (in his refusal to grasp the meaning of his father's mercy and love) who has become the unrepentant sinner!*

From a biblical perspective, no one seems to have a better grasp of the issues that pertain to the meaning of human life than St. Paul. His understanding of the purpose of Jesus' suffering, death, and resurrection enabled him to transform his suffering into joy. This is the spiritual equivalent of turning garbage into treasure.

> Even now I find my joy in the suffering I endure. . . . In my own flesh I fill up what is lacking in the sufferings of Christ for the sake of his body, the church (Col 1:24).

The most practical reason to follow Paul's example of relating life's meaning and purpose to Jesus is that suffering is inevitable; neither complaints nor escapism can take it away. In the end we have only two choices: we can suffer and complain, or we can transform our suffering into joy by giving it the meaning and purpose that God intends.

Paul's emphasis on the redemptive value of suffering has influenced my own perspective. I used to ask: "Why do roses have thorns?" Now I'm wondering whether it's better to ask: "Why do thorns have roses?"

The beatitudes (Mt 5:3–12) provide excellent clues to the sources of life's meaning; the key words are:

poor in spirit
sorrowing
lowly
hunger and thirst for holiness
show mercy
single-hearted

peacemakers
holiness
persecution and slander

If the above words characterize your choices, you're on the right path. To stay on that path, keep your energies focused on the achievement of spiritual unity with God and neighbor. In short, if you want to give deep meaning to your life, be a disciple of Jesus.

Once you have learned to keep the sources of life's meaning in focus, it becomes easier to deal with the problems that pleasure creates. The first is that pleasure is so attractive that it takes self-control to resist overindulgence. In the play "Tribute," Jack Lemmon played a fun-loving comedian named "Scottie." Scottie was a terminal cancer patient. His illness caused him to look back at the meaning of his life, particularly at his divorce and his tempestuous relationship with his son. Scottie played the role of comedian to the end, but in one of his philosophical moments he shared a meaningful insight: "Nothing needs less justification than pleasure."

A second problem with pleasure is that its seductive nature frequently creates an addiction similar to that associated with drugs and alcohol. Jesus warned his disciples:

> Be on guard lest your spirits become bloated with indulgence and drunkenness and worldly cares. The great day will suddenly close in on you like a trap. The day I speak of will come upon all who dwell on the face of the earth. So be on the watch (Lk 21:34–36).

Jesus' exhortation to vigilance is a reminder that all of us are accountable to God for what we are doing with our time, talent, and treasure. Grace is the best cure for addictive behavior.

A third problem is that since pleasure is a temporal experience, its pay-off is so quick that it tends to distract us from spiritual opportunities (which suffer from the costs associated with delayed gratification). Things haven't changed much. Paul wrote that "unbelieving minds have been blinded by the god of the present age so that they do not see the splendor of the gospel showing forth in the glory of Christ, the image of God" (2 Cor 4:4). Pleasure is at least as much the "god of the present age" today as it was then; in fact, advances in science and technology are making pleasure a more attractive idol than it has ever been.

Because pleasure is not intrinsically sinful, we do not have to reject the things of this world. Indeed, "re-creation" is desirable for our physical, emotional, and spiritual well-being. Although we need not give up everything, we ought to be willing to give up *any*-thing that damages our relationships with God and neighbor.

Jesus gave the disciples some practical advice regarding the right use of money and temporal goods and pleasures:

> Make friends for yourselves through your use of this world's goods, so that when they fail you, a lasting reception will be yours (Lk 16:9).

> No servant can serve two masters. Either he will hate the one and love the other, or be attentive to the one and despise the other. You cannot give yourself to God and money (Lk 16:13).

Eventually, all pleasures will fade away. All of our temporal goods will eventually be consumed by rust, corrosion, and decay. What we do manage to hold onto until death will still pass to someone else. After death, those who have spent too much time and energy searching for pleasure will be left clutching the proverbial "empty bag."

The best way to strike a healthy balance is to allow Jesus to give meaning to our lives. As Jesus entered Jerusalem for the last time before the crucifixion, he said something that, on the surface, is not easy to understand. "The man who loves his life loses it, while the man who hates his life in this world preserves it to life eternal" (Jn 12:25). *This verse is confusing unless we link life's meaning with love and spirituality;* Jesus' message is that because the meaning of human life is spiritual, all temporal realities ("life in this world") are secondary.

Table 19.1 summarizes this chapter and lists some of the characteristics that distinguish meaning from pleasure.

Table 19.1

From: Pleasure	To: Meaning
Spending/keeping	Giving
Receiving	Serving others
Drown out the pain	"No pain, no gain" (the Christian experience of pain is redemptive)
Instant gratification	Delay of gratification
Being entertained	Visiting the sick
Overeating	Fasting/giving up candy for Lent
Passive	Active
Low energy level	High energy level
Temporal needs tend to grow at the expense of spiritual needs.	Spiritual needs come first.
Watching insipid TV programs	Watching educational TV programs
Self-centered	God-centered
Temptations reveal the presence of evil.	Beatitudes reveal the presence of God.
Envy	Joy

CHAPTER TWENTY

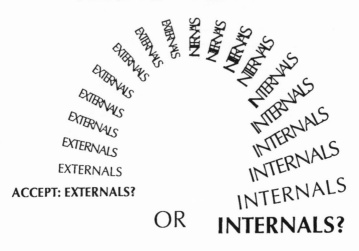

ACCEPT: EXTERNALS?

OR **INTERNALS?**

The days are coming . . . when I will make a new covenant
with the house of Israel and the house of Judah. It will not be
like the covenant I made with their fathers. . . . But this is the
covenant I will make. . . . I will place my law within them, and
write it upon their hearts . . . (Jer 31:31–33).

The significance of accepting internals is that the spiritual
transformation that faith leads to occurs from *within*. Jesus described the grace of baptism as an internal fountain that provides eternal life:

Whoever drinks the water I give him will never be thirsty; no,
the water I give shall become a fountain within him leaping up
to provide eternal life (Jn 4:14).

As we allow the Holy Spirit to transform us from the inside-out, we can overcome the limitations of the ten commandments (which can only provide guidance from the outside-in). It is far better to develop the positive life-giving mentality that flows from the indwelling presence of the Holy Spirit (a lifestyle that asks: What can I *give* you?) than to regard the ten commandments as a *constraint*.

The primary danger of trying to enforce obedience to any external law—including the ten commandments—is that of legalism. Consider the dispute that arose early in the church's history regarding the necessity of circumcision. Because Jewish law required it of all males, it was eventually regarded as a sign of faith, even for *Gentile* converts to Christianity! Paul's response was:

> Appearance does not make a Jew. True circumcision is not a sign in the flesh. He is a real Jew who is one inwardly, and true circumcision is of the heart; its source is the spirit, not the letter (Rom 2:28–29).

Legalistic people tend to cling to laws that are no longer necessary because they want to hold on to what is familiar and comfortable. Whereas faith is "internal" because it is a gift "of the heart," legalism, which is born of our need for security, is intrinsically "heartless" and therefore incapable of supporting the gratuity called "love."

The old covenant, which was based on keeping the ten commandments, ultimately failed; it could not give mankind enough internal power to comply. In contrast, the new covenant, which was sealed by the blood that Christ shed on the cross, can provide an everlasting source of internal grace-power to those who use their freedom to act out their trust in God. Paul's disdain for the written law of the old covenant reached its peak by the time of his third missionary journey:

> God . . . has made us qualified ministers of a new covenant, a
> covenant not of written law but of spirit. The written law kills,
> but the Spirit gives life (2 Cor 3:6).

The Spirit which unites us in the body of Christ is the driving
force that accounts for the uniqueness of human life. The more
we cooperate with the Spirit, the more the church can succeed
in becoming the sacramental sign of God's love for mankind.

If we displace God and his internal grace-power with externals, even religious externals, we can come dangerously close to
turning religion into just another human activity. This is what
Jesus had in mind when he responded to the Pharisees and
"experts" in the law who asked him why his disciples did not go
through the Jewish ritual of purifying their hands before eating.
Jesus called them "hypocrites" (Mk 7:1–23); then he added:
"Nothing that enters a man from outside can make him impure;
that which comes out of him, and only that, constitutes impu-
rity" (Mk 7:15).

Ephesians 3 contains a prayer that emphasizes the internal
dimension of mature faith.

> May he [God the Father] strengthen you inwardly through
> the working of the Spirit. May Christ dwell in your hearts
> through faith, and may charity be the route and foundation
> of your life. Thus you will be able to grasp fully . . . the
> breadth and length and height and depth of Christ's love, and
> experience this love which surpasses all knowledge, so that
> you may attain to the fullness of God himself (Eph 3:16–19).

When we have enough trust in God to place his will above our
own, the Holy Spirit's indwelling presence transforms the quality of our lives as we are drawn closer and closer to the fullness
of Christ's divinity.

In contrast to "internals," which directly reflect the disposition of the inner person toward God, "externals" merely describe outward appearances. Job titles, military rank, wealth, possessions, and the "masks" that people wear are common examples of "externals." The suicides of celebrities testify to the fact that too often people who *appear* to have everything on the outside are empty on the inside.

Anything we have been taught is also an "external." Even the ten commandments serve only as a map; they can help us to choose the right path, but they cannot provide the internal strength we need to complete our spiritual journey. The attractiveness of "externals" stems primarily from their quick pay-off. In our temporal lives it is seductively easy to use them to wear the appearances of success and competence. Similarly, in our religious lives we can self-righteously obey the laws of our choosing, while finding convenient loopholes for laws that we would rather not obey.

By definition, "externals" allow manipulation or control to be exerted by an outside force. The completeness of our freedom to choose makes it obvious that God doesn't manipulate us; instead, he has offered us the opportunity to become adopted sons and daughters—who respond by freely choosing to embody his message of *love*. Over-reliance on externals is an abuse of the freedom God gave us as creatures who bear his image and likeness.

The scribes and Pharisees stifled their personal growth by adding—and then becoming preoccupied with—the "external" of 613 precepts of the law. As a result, Jesus had to warn his disciples: "Unless your holiness surpasses that of the scribes and Pharisees you shall not enter the kingdom of God" (Mt 5:20). Listen to the harsh tone in Jesus' words of criticism:

> Woe to you scribes and Pharisees, you frauds! You cleanse the outside of the cup and dish, and fill the inside with loot and lust (Mt 23:25).

> Woe to you scribes and Pharisees, you frauds! You are like
> whitewashed tombs, beautiful to look at on the outside but
> inside full of filth and dead men's bones (Mt 23:27).

Read Matthew 23 in its entirety to grasp just how angry Jesus
was when he called them a "vipers' nest" and a "brood of ser-
pents" (v. 33).

The early church was not immune to tensions and conflict
over similar issues. Since many initial converts were Jewish, a
conflict soon arose over whether non-Jewish males who wished
to be baptized should be circumcised first. Paul, a former Phari-
see and a circumcised Jew, argued against this external religious
practice in favor of the internal disposition of faith. "In Christ
Jesus neither circumcision nor lack of it counts for anything;
only faith, which expresses itself through love" (Gal 5:6). Unless
external religious practices are accompanied by the proper interior dispositions, they run the risk of becoming sterile.

Paul's argument against circumcision is based on his own
experience of the limitations of religious practices based on
externals.

> If anyone thinks he has a right to put his trust on external
> evidence, all the more can I! I was circumcised on the eighth
> day . . . in legal observance I was a Pharisee, and so zealous
> that I persecuted the church. I was above reproach when it
> came to justice based on the law. But those things I used to
> consider gain I have now reappraised as loss in the light of
> Christ (Phil 3:4–7).

Our salvation is not based on observance of the letter of any
law—even the ten commandments; in Paul's words, "we are
released from the law, dead to what held us captive, so that we
may serve in the newness of the spirit and not under the obso-

lete letter" (Rom 7:6). *Salvation is a gift from God, who, by breathing his power into us, powers us out of captivity to sin and death.*

Externals, such as possessions, masks, or legalistic dependence on religious laws, bring only temporary satisfaction. *Joy,* which lasts far longer, is the result of an indwelling of the Holy Spirit and is revealed by the good habits and positive attitudes that theologians call virtues.

At one time or another, almost all of us submit to the temptation to wear masks. When we are afraid, we may wear the mask of toughness; when we are insecure, we may wear the mask of success. If such pretense is allowed to become habitual, it will require constant vigilance. The wearing of masks can also make it difficult to enjoy work. According to Maxwell Maltz in *Psycho-Cybernetics,* "The most miserable and tortured people in the world are those who are continually straining and striving to convince themselves and others that they are something other than what they basically are." Many masks are worn to conform to the roles that are attached to jobs in hierarchies. In Erich Fromm's words in *To Have Or To Be:*

> In most larger and hierarchically organized societies the process of alienation of authority occurs. . . . Competence is transferred to the uniform or to the title. . . . This external sign of competence replaces the real competence and its qualities.

Titles and roles become attractive when they confer either money or power over others. Sometimes they become attractive because of peer pressure. But the cost is too high, for role-playing and the wearing of masks inevitably generate anxiety. Merton in *The New Man* described the frustration that results from the wearing of masks by describing contentment with exterior identity as "spiritual disaster."

It all boils down to this: God sees through externals to what is hidden deep within our hearts; since he has created us in his image and likeness, what he ought to see is a reflection of himself.

Table 20.1 summarizes this chapter by listing some of the characteristics that distinguish internals from externals.

Table 20.1

From: Externals	To: Internals
Masks/pretense	Who I really am/the real me
Titles/roles define who I am.	Relationships with God & neighbor define who I am.
Beating one's breast as a symbol of unworthiness	All my actions reflect reverence for God.
Grace is something I "get" from outside.	Grace powers me from within.
The ten commandments/canon law	Embracing God's truth/values in my heart (cf. Jer 31:34)/I *am* a temple of the Holy Spirit.

Religiosity
  Conflict and division
	Spirituality
	  Peace, joy and integrity

CHAPTER TWENTY-ONE

RESPOND: ATTACHMENT?

OR COMMITMENT?

I must be baptized, and how great is my anguish until it is accomplished (Lk 12:50).

Commitment as "true grit" flows from deep within us and has the potential to reveal our most meaningful—and costly—gifts. The cost is measured by the attachments we give up. Years ago the Franciscan Communication Center in Los Angeles produced a series of thirty-second "Telespots" that some commercial television stations aired as a public service. One of them depicted a woman taking care of someone lying on the ground in abject poverty. A solemn voice in the background said: "I wouldn't do that for a million dollars." The woman, wearing a simple white robe and a glowing smile, turned her head and replied, "Neither would I."

Commitment springs from love, and love from the will to nurture spiritual growth. Even though Jesus expressed anguish over his impending crucifixion and death, he persevered in his commitment because he *knew* that after the Holy Spirit came upon the disciples at Pentecost, the sacrificial meaning and purpose of his life would emerge with astonishing clarity. For Christians, commitment, love, and spiritual life become inseparable.

Commitments to God tend to focus on:

1. meaning more than pleasure
2. "internals" more than "externals"

The more committed we are to God, the more likely we will share gifts with those who are hungry, or thirsty, or needy, or in prison. None of this would be possible without "grace," the power we receive when we are willing to act in partnership with God.

Because Jesus embodies the fullness of God's revelation to mankind, the single most important commitment we can make is to be his follower. The body of Christ is not a religious institution; it is an organism made up of personal relationships. All institutions, including the Catholic Church, are constantly challenged to overcome the adverse effects of bureaucracy, especially impersonal behavior. Ideally, people who attend religious rituals do so to give expression to the meaning of their lives. Hopefully they expect the communion and community that is the focal point of our celebration of eucharist to exist before, during, and after it is over. If it is not, the Church's visibility as a "light to the world" is obscured, and in the resulting darkness the probability of complacency increases dramatically. *Our goal ought not be to make religion more personal, but our lives more committed as expressions of spiritual growth and renewal.*

The body of Christ is both the collective effect of our personal commitments to God, and the source of the unity that bonds us; only in this body can we gain the strength to endure the pain and suffering that inevitably lies ahead. Thus Jesus called us to be refreshed *together:*

> Come to me, all you who are weary and find life burdensome, and I will refresh you. Take my yoke upon your shoulders and learn from me, for I am gentle and humble of heart. Your souls will find rest, for my yoke is easy, and my burden light (Mt 11:28–30).

The more personal our relationship to God, the easier it is to place his will above our own. Submission to God brings with it a divine promise that our sufferings are well-fitted to our needs, and that our lives will be filled with meaning and purpose and strength.

Disciples who are committed to Jesus:

1. express Christian values with conviction
2. are willing to accept the suffering and death into which they were plunged/baptized
3. are concerned with the needs of others

The more committed we are to God, the more likely we are to become neighbors with people who would have otherwise remained strangers. Some of our new neighbors will be hungry. Some will be thirsty. Some will be ill, and some even in prison. All of them bear God's image and likeness; when we serve them we are also serving Jesus.

I often ask people who come in for counseling to describe their relationship with Jesus. Their responses are usually confused and vague, and generally boil down to going or not going to church. The quality of our relationship with anyone—especially God—is better manifested by the closeness that results from commitment and good communication than by how often we "go" to church.

The depraved crimes committed by participants in devil worship reflect their estrangement from God. Their behavior is so self-destructive that it often involves extreme risk; relatively few people can survive very long at a level that is so impoverished that communication with God is expressed as hatred. *However, even those who express mere indifference to God end up wounding themselves in the process.*

Because spiritual apathy lies between the extremes of love and hate, it seems harmless. *Do not be fooled!* It can quickly turn into a deadly sin. Its symptoms include domestic violence, crime, or drug addiction. In short, apathy is a divisive force that acts like a cancer by breaking down our relationships with God and neighbor. It is the antithesis of the unity which God has ordained for the church. Apathy, as an impersonal response to God, can evolve into a sin of mammoth proportions.

Because of the effects of bureaucracy, all large organizations, *including the church,* provide a convenient and comfortable dwelling place for apathetic people. People who live and work in large institutions can hide behind rules and laws—making them an end in themselves—instead of a means to the end of service. The following story illustrates the gradual and insidious process through which this inversion takes place.

> On a rocky seacoast where shipwrecks were frequent there was once a ramshackle little life-saving station. It was no more than a shack and there was only one boat. But the few people who manned the station were devoted and kept constant watch over the sea; with little regard for themselves and their safety, they went fearlessly out in a storm if they had any evidence that there had been a shipwreck somewhere. Many lives were thus saved and the station became famous.

As the reputation of the station grew, so did the desire of people in the neighborhood to become associated with its excellent work. They generously offered of their time and money, so new members were enrolled, new boats bought, and new crews trained. The shack was replaced by a comfortable building that could adequately handle the needs of those who had been saved from the sea, and since shipwrecks do not occur every day, it became a popular gathering place—a sort of local club.

As time passed the members became so engaged in socializing that they had little interest in lifesaving, though they still sported the lifesaving motto on the badges they wore. As a matter of fact, when some people were actually rescued from the sea, it was always such a nuisance because they were dirty and sick and soiled the carpeting and furniture.

Soon the social activities of the club became so numerous and the lifesaving activities so few that there was a showdown at a club meeting; some members insisted that they return to their original purpose and activity. A vote was taken and those trouble makers, who proved to be a small minority, were invited to leave the club and start another.

Which is precisely what they did—a little further down the coast, with such selflessness and daring that, after a while, their heroism made them famous. Whereupon their membership was enlarged, their hut reconstructed—and their idealism smothered. If you happen to visit that area today, you will find a number of exclusive clubs dotting the shoreline. Each one is still justifiably proud of its origin and its tradition. When shipwrecks occur in those parts today, nobody seems to care.

There are only two alternatives. We can either allow attachments and comfortable behavior to become the norm, or be committed to serve others as members of the body of Christ. If we choose the former, the pleasures afforded by technological progress may eventually become irresistible. If we choose the latter, personal relationships with God and neighbor will keep generating healing power and new life; the gifts that result are the subject of the next chapter.

Table 21.1 summarizes this chapter by listing some of the characteristics that distinguish commitment from attachment.

Table 21.1

From: Attachment	To: Commitment
Codependence (I control you, or allow your behavior to control me.)	Healthy relationships are based on *freedom.*
Others make me *happy.*	*Joy* comes from serving others.
Clinging to: —things/money (greed) —guilt (scrupulosity) —fantasy (pretending instead of doing)	Actions are *life-giving* when: —people come before possessions —love displaces guilt —I *do* something
Comfort, apathy	Vitality
Infatuation: —love *feels* so good —religious rituals *feel* so good	Love: —puts *sacrifice* above self-gratification —it is tough to fulfill the "significance" of sacraments
Impulsive	Count the cost, choose, then don't look back!
Hard to give up	Hard to fulfill

CHAPTER TWENTY-TWO

COMPULSION COMPULSION COMPULSION COMPULSION COMPULSION COMPULSION COMPULSION COMPULSION COMPULSION
GIFTS GIFTS GIFTS GIFTS GIFTS GIFTS GIFTS GIFTS GIFTS GIFTS GIFTS

EXPRESS: COMPULSION?

OR

GIFTS?

Mary said, ". . . I am the handmaid of the Lord. May it be done to me according to your word." Then the angel departed from her (Lk 1:38).

Gifts, as expressions of commitment, are incompatible with compulsion; when exchanged by Spirit-filled people, gifts become magnificent expressions of the vitality of the body of Christ and the supernatural consequence of God's grace-power. They give life meaning and purpose, and make it worth living.

God has given each of us unique gifts to share; when we are not "graced," we may compulsively hide them out of fear or even "ab-use" them in an exploitive manner. When they are neither abused nor buried, they become the building blocks of Christian communities.

> We have gifts that differ according to the favor bestowed on each of us. One's gift may be prophecy; its use should be in proportion to his faith. It may be the gift of ministry; it should be used for service. One who is a teacher should use his gift for teaching; one with the power of exhortation should exhort. He who gives alms should do so generously; he who rules should exercise his authority with care; he who performs works of mercy should do so cheerfully (Rom 12:6–8).

Because we are free, our generosity as givers is an outward expression of our inner disposition. God wants us to be cheerful givers (see 2 Cor 9:7). Our work and even our hobbies can provide excellent opportunities to spread joy and to reveal God's meaning to a world that is spiritually hungry. As the spirit of generous and cheerful giving spreads, it becomes an outward sign of the unity that is an essential property of the dynamic church.

The greatest gift we can give to God is our will. Abraham submitted to the will of God on Mount Moriah (Gen 22:1–19). Mary submitted to the will of God in the annunciation (Lk 1:38). Jesus submitted to the will of the Father in the garden of Gethsemane (Lk 22:42). Giving and receiving God's gifts touches the essence of what it means to be a person of faith and produces the supernatural connectivity that bonds us in the body of Christ.

Because the gifts that we are being called to share in a cheerful manner may lie beneath the surface of our consciousness, God will help us to discover them. "The Spirit we have received is not the world's spirit, but God's Spirit helping us to recognize the gifts he has given us" (1 Cor 2:12). When we share Christian gifts, we are helping others by helping ourselves. While the spiritual gifts that God has entrusted to our care may not seem valuable when compared to the value that society places on athletic ability or the ability to perform on stage, in fact they have an infinite value.

Prophecy has a special place among the gifts of the Holy Spirit because it contributes heavily to the building up of the church. "Set your hearts on spiritual gifts—above all the gift of prophecy" (1 Cor 14:1). Prophets are less predictors of the future then they are proclaimers of God's Word. Because what they say is so deeply rooted in the Spirit it is literally *full* of truth; when we look back, their words often appear to have been successful predictions.

Prophecy is the natural consequence of being baptized—of being God's friend. Speaking for God is a form of ministry. While the manner in which our individual ministries should be carried out may differ, the Holy Spirit will fashion unity out of our diversity.

> There are different gifts but the same Spirit; there are different ministries but the same Lord; there are different works but the same God who accomplishes all of them in everyone. To each person the manifestation is given for the common good (1 Cor 12:4–7).

May God's will be done through us as communities of believers.

Failure to use our spiritual gifts is serious enough to be a matter of sin. Indeed, some of our greatest sins may be those of omission. These sins, which are generally the result of fears and laziness, weaken the whole church and are repugnant to God! Read Matthew 25:14–30. The master, who represents God, is extremely negative toward the fearful servant: "You worthless, lazy lout!" (v. 26). A lout is a person who is scorned, an awkward stupid person, an oaf. Because this was one of the last stories that Jesus told his disciples before he went to Jerusalem for his crucifixion, it takes on even greater significance. God must have great expectations for the people he has prepared for ministry:

When much has been given a man, much will be required of
him. More will be asked of a man to whom more has been
entrusted. I have come to light a fire on the earth. How I wish
the blaze were ignited (Lk 12:48–49).

Jesus lit a fire when he suffered and died, and then rose from
the dead; and on the first Pentecost the Holy Spirit transformed
it into a blaze.

Abusing God's gifts, out of either greed or fear, ultimately
leads to dissension and resentment. When the mother of the
apostles James and John approached Jesus with an ambitious
and selfish goal, Jesus directed her thoughts to *service*. They
wanted a special place in Jesus' kingdom. Jesus tried to explain
to them that they did not know what they were asking for, because in his kingdom "anyone among you who aspires to greatness must serve the rest" (Mt 20:26). The more we attempt to
give to others, the more Christlike, hence the more harmonious
and integral our growth becomes. Such growth is "harmonious" because it coordinates our interdependent functioning
within the body of Christ, and "integral" because it makes
us whole.

Any sound tree bears good fruit, while a decayed tree bears
bad fruit. A sound tree cannot bear bad fruit any more than a
decayed tree can bear good fruit. Every tree that does not
bear good fruit is cut down and thrown into the fire. You can
tell a tree by its fruit (Mt 7:17–20).

Our generosity in sharing our God-given gifts measures our
prophetic response to God better than any other because "actions speak louder than words." When we die, God is not likely
to ask us how many times we missed mass, or how many religious
rules we broke; he is far more likely to ask: "What did you do
with the gifts I gave you?" Spirit-actualizing people use their

creative power to keep finding appropriate opportunities to serve others; their reward is God's peace, and a life filled with meaning and purpose.

By being and acting as givers/ministers who are partners with God, we can experience a joy and peace that sheds new light on the passing pleasures that this world affords. Human beings were created to live in a communion of mind and heart with God and one another; this is what it means to say that the church is the body of Christ. With Christ as our head, we are being called to live in perfect harmony, each giving and receiving according to God's will.

Failure to express our faith through the giving and receiving of Christian gifts creates a vacuum that may soon be filled with compulsive behaviors such as:

1. attachments to things, substances, or people, e.g. greed, addictions to drugs or alcohol, or codependence (a co-dependent person is one who has let another person's behavior affect him or her, and who may become obsessed with controlling that person's behavior)
2. legalism and strict adherence to a fixed ideology

Legalism and fixed ideologies stifle life in the Spirit by diverting attention away from commitments to develop and share of our God-given gifts, and toward compliance with policies, procedures, and rules. Keep the lesson of Matthew 25:14–30 clearly in mind! The steward who buried his talents out of fear was afraid that he would be punished for making a bad investment. He was even too afraid to lend the money at interest. Every time we bury a talent out of fear, countless numbers of people suffer by being deprived of gifts that God wants them to receive. Obligations leave little room for gift-giving, and lives dominated by obligations are less than fully human. Obligations work best for robots who have no freedom, no character, no feelings, and no growth potential; *people* who subject themselves to unnecessary constraints face a similar threat.

Where relationships express love and commitment, the sharing of gifts enhances community life and lightens life's burdens. The sharing of gifts reunites people who have suffered from the divisive effects of greed, substance addiction, codependence, and legalism. When tensions increase our anxieties, our need for pleasure also increases, and the vicious circle of anxiety feeds on itself. If we emphasize *giving* to others in all spheres of human life—including the temporal—the Spirit of justice and truth can serve as the means of human "quality control."

After I read *The Neurotic Personality of Our Time* by Karen Horney, I felt uncomfortable because I realized that my behavior had some neurotic elements. Education and experience have confirmed that many of the greatest threats we face come from within. As Maslow states in *Motivation and Personality*, "Most neurotic symptoms . . . amount to basic-need-gratification bent impulses that have somehow got stymied or fixated on the wrong means." If our vision is not fixed on God (the right means), we tend to drift compulsively toward the "wrong means" called sinfulness.

There are so many unknowns in our environment that it is easy to feel threatened. Indeed, the more adventurous we become, the more unknowns we will have to face. The best way to deal with such threats is to do our best, and then trust God. Because our sinful nature predisposes us to choose the wrong means (compulsive reliance on self), our spiritual health depends on grace.

To fully comprehend what it means to call faith a "gift" is to acknowledge God's initiative by responding in kind—by sharing the gracious fruits of his indwelling Spirit with others.

Table 22.1 summarizes this chapter by listing some of the characteristics that distinguish gifts from compulsion.

Table 22.1

From: Compulsion	To: Gifts
Addictions (drugs, alcoholism, workaholism, etc.)	Freedom of choice
Codependence (I control you, or allow your behavior to control me)	Mutual integrity
Decay	Renewal
"Bad fruit"	"Good fruit"
Conflicts (with self or others)	Tranquility
Temporal needs are dominant.	Spiritual life is dominant.
Spiritual paralysis	Prophecy expresses each person's unique gifts.
No control/no discipline	The Spirit guides/makes "disciples"
Weakness	Power
Destruction	Creation
Competitive	Non-competitive
Self-serving/selfish	Serve others/generous
No motivation to share anything	Sharing gives meaning to my life
No good news means there's nothing to evangelize.	Evangelization is an expression of gratitude.

CHAPTER TWENTY-THREE

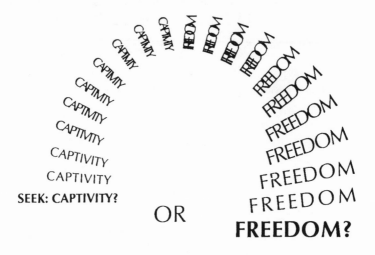

SEEK: CAPTIVITY? OR **FREEDOM?**

Now the Lord is the Spirit,
and where the Spirit of the Lord is,
there is freedom (2 Cor 3:17).

Few people ever seek captivity, but many are unconsciously being held captive by experiences that bring intense pleasure, or by a compulsive need to find "the answer." And all of us are caught in the grip of original sin. Until we recognize our captivity, we are not unlikely to appreciate baptism's most unique gift—freedom from all captivity, even the trauma associated with death!

"The Lord is the Spirit, and where the Spirit of the Lord is, there is freedom." Here's the catch: the freedom that God offers can only be experienced by those who are willing to submit to God's will, and his will is that we become baptismal participants in his suffering and death. True freedom is not the freedom to "do our thing," it is the freedom to become more Christlike; this means that we ought to begin thinking of miracles less in terms of God doing our will, and more in terms of *acting like Jesus.*

Jesus never made any misleading promises about the cost of freedom and discipleship; indeed his commission has always been incredibly frank:

> Be on your way, and remember: I am sending you as lambs in the midst of wolves (Lk 10:3).

The cross offers us the opportunity to fulfill our human potential—but only by confronting the "wolves" who are dispersed throughout our baptismal bath of pain and suffering.

Because we have the advantage of hindsight, our "desert experiences" should be less traumatic than the ancient Israelites' were. When you are discouraged, read Exodus 14, beginning at verse 11:

> They complained to Moses, "Were there no burial places in Egypt that you had to bring us out here to die in the desert? Why did you do this to us? Why did you bring us out of Egypt?

Moses replied: "The Lord himself will fight for you; you have only to keep still."

Paradoxically, Christian freedom comes from *dependence*— on God. In *The New Man* Merton states:

> The free man is the one whose choices have given him the power to stand on his own feet and determine his own life according to the higher light and spirit that are in him. The

slave, in the spiritual order, is the man whose choices have
destroyed all spontaneity in him and have delivered him over,
bound hand and foot, to his own compulsions, idiosyncracies,
and illusions, so that he never does what he really wants to do.
His spirit is not in command. . . . He is commanded by his
own weak flesh and its passions—fear, greed, lust, insecurity,
untruthfulness, envy, cruelty-servility, and all the rest.

The American appetite for freedom is becoming increasingly
self-centered. Now, more than ever, the world needs the church's
"light" a light that can shine only if we, as the body of Christ,
exercise our freedom by:

1. prayerfully accepting God's insight;
2. after being informed by the Spirit of truth, turn ourselves
   inside out by serving others.

The source of the "higher light and freedom" that Merton uses
to describe people who are free is the Spirit of truth that Jesus
first breathed into the church at Pentecost. The next chapter
will focus on the role the Holy Spirit plays in the church as we
journey from illusions to the holiness of truth.

Table 23.1 summarizes this chapter by listing some of the
characteristics that distinguish freedom from captivity.

Table 23.1

From: Captivity	To: Freedom
Change causes anxiety	Change is a sign of growth and renewal.
I must control my life	I must submit to the will of God.
Revenge	Forgiveness
I can't let you discover who I really am.	Living without deceit
Greed—always wanting: new car, new house, more money, *etc.*	Contentment
Grabbing institutional/ organizational power	Becoming a better servant
Exercising too much	Exercising adequately
Dieting too little/too much	Balanced diet
Feeling "trapped"	Feeling liberated to develop talents/gifts
Inability to choose/decide	It's OK to make mistakes.
It's hopeless. There's too much pain.	I can endure pain and suffering.
I'm not responsible for my feelings.	What I think determines how I feel.
"Poor me"/self-pity	I am a child of God!
Death is the end.	Life is eternal.
Substance abuse (addictions to drugs or alcohol)	Prudent use
I experience constant feelings of guilt.	Love erases guilt.
"Needing" someone/inability to live without someone	Choosing to love
What will others think?	Selecting the best alternative
I'll do it later.	I'll do it now.

CHAPTER TWENTY-FOUR

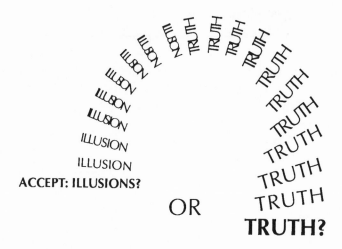

ACCEPT: ILLUSIONS?

OR

TRUTH?

If you remain in my word, you will truly be my disciples, and you will know the truth, and the truth will set you free (Jn 8:31–32).

If we adopt St. Augustine's perspective of seeing spiritual life as "a series of conversions to truth," the best place to begin a journey away from illusions is in the Old Testament's book of Wisdom. By personifying wisdom as a "kindly spirit" (Wis 1:6), and giving God's wisdom a life of its own, the author sets the stage for our understanding of the Holy Spirit.

> For she is the refulgence of eternal light,
>   the spotless mirror of the power of God,
>   the image of his goodness.

And she, who is one, can do all things,
  and renews everything while herself perduring.
And passing into holy souls from age to age,
  she produces friends of God and prophets (Wis 7:26–27).

Our baptismal conversion to truth occurs when the indwelling presence of the Holy Spirit changes us into "friends of God *and prophets.*" Prophecy is the apex of human freedom because the role of a prophet is to proclaim God's truth.

The sacraments serve as the means of our ongoing conversion and the source of the grace that energizes us for the prophetic task. Paul wrote, "Our preaching of the gospel provided not a mere matter of words for you but one of power; it was carried on in the Holy Spirit and out of complete conviction" (1 Thes 1:5). Do not be misled by the minimal requirements of religion. Our vocation is not to be "religious," it is to receive God's powerful Word with an open mind, and to be sufficiently animated by his Spirit to act on it with sacramentality and "conviction." Thus Jesus prayed:

Consecrate them by means of truth—
"Your word is truth."
As you have sent me into the world,
so I have sent them into the world;
I consecrate myself for their sakes now,
that they may be consecrated in truth (Jn 17:17–19).

The purpose of our consecration is not to take on the appearance of holiness, but to *act* with the unique authority and freedom that is generated by the indwelling of God's truthful Spirit.

From the moment we accept and internalize the Spirit of truth, we will begin to gain deeper and deeper insight into the meaning and purpose of life. Legalistic observance of religious

laws and passive attendance at rituals may make us *feel* good—
without ever producing the spiritual renewal we need to achieve
harmonious and integral growth. As Merton says in *The New
Man:*

> A spirit of servile conformity to rites and precepts, without
> the interior commitment of our whole selves to the conse-
> quences of a moral choice, obstructs the interior action of
> grace and prevents us from establishing a vital contact with
> the invisible Spirit of God. And by that very fact it prevents
> from finding our true selves in the actualization of our own
> deepest capacity for charity and self-consecration. But in
> order to interiorize our spiritual activity we have to develop
> our awareness of spiritual realities. And this spiritual aware-
> ness, which depends first of all on faith, is also impossible if
> we do not have a genuine knowledge of ourselves.

We cannot come to a genuine knowledge of ourselves without
first understanding that the only choice that can make us whole
is a decision that commits us to accept and internalize the Spirit
of truth. Faith becomes a living expression of integrity or
wholeness only when we allow God to touch us *from within.*

God's Word is to illusion what light is to darkness; the closer
our relationship to Jesus, the greater our capacity to appreciate
the limitations of affluence:

> Do not store up for yourselves treasures on earth, where
> moth and decay destroy, and thieves break in and steal. But
> store up treasures in heaven, where neither moth nor decay
> destroy, nor thieves break in and steal (Mt 6:19–20).

Instead of traveling to far-away places to experience the peace
and tranquility that reflect God's truth, we ought to embrace it
and proclaim it—and thereby make it more visible at home.

While others may think we are foolish for doing so, we can take comfort in Noah's example; after the floods came, he looked a lot smarter!

Table 24.1 summarizes this chapter by listing some of the characteristics that distinguish truth from illusions.

Table 24.1

From: Illusions	To: Truth
Problems can be covered up/hidden.	Problems can get worse.
If people knew who I really am, they wouldn't like me.	Christian love is unconditional.
Life is fair.	Life is *not* fair.
I deserve more than this.	Life is difficult.
I'm too old.	I'm only as old as I feel.
When your "time is up," you die.	Death is the result of human freedom and the laws of nature.
God punishes me when I'm bad.	When I sin, I punish myself by damaging my relationship with God.
It's OK to lie.	Lying damages my integrity.
I have to earn what I get from God.	God loves me; when I am at my best, I *reflect* the image and likeness of God.
I don't have any sins to confess.	Having an informed conscience keeps me from straying far from Jesus.
It's better to avoid certain subjects. It's better to suppress unpleasant feelings.	Truth strengthens relationships.
Love conquers all.	Love makes me vulnerable.
I can do it better myself.	We need each other.
My religious beliefs are private.	I am a prophet/spokesperson for God.
I am powerless	The Holy Spirit enlightens/empowers me from within.

CHAPTER TWENTY-FIVE

RESPOND: PRIDE?   OR   **RELATIONSHIP?**

PRIDE / PRIDE / PRIDE / PRIDE / PRIDE / PRIDE / PRIDE / PRIDE / PRIDE / RELATIONSHIP / RELATIONSHIP / RELATIONSHIP / RELATIONSHIP / RELATIONSHIP / RELATIONSHIP / RELATIONSHIP / RELATIONSHIP / RELATIONSHIP / RELATIONSHIP

I am the vine, you are the branches. Whoever remains in me and I in him will bear much fruit, because without me you can do nothing (Jn 15:5).

People who suffer from pride are often portrayed in a humorous fashion by the media. My favorite proud characters—and they certainly were "characters"—are: Ralph Kramden, Archie Bunker, Ted Baxter, Frank Burns, and Charles Emerson Winchester III. Their behavior has at least one of the following roots:

1. the personal satisfaction they derive from what *they* achieve (measured by their own fixed standard—a creed that makes *them* comfortable)

2. the satisfaction *they* derive from *their* job title or position

Because pride leaves little room for the truth that forms the foundation for relationships, it is not compatible with the relationship called "salvation."

Pride is rarely as funny in the real world as it is on television. The turmoil and alienation that characterize our time are a sign that relationships with God and with one another are not healthy. The root cause of the problems that divide us is the same: it is the spiritual "dis-ease" that results when individuals do not relate well to God. Pride is the antithesis of spirituality because it is too *self*-centered; it becomes the root of all evil by fooling us into thinking that we can *earn* God's love as a reward for being "good."

Turmoil and disorder are not new to mankind; the Old Testament records the heroic struggle of the prophets to call a troubled people to repentance for their sins. In the end, disobedience of the ten commandments shattered the old covenant; with this breakdown, the rituals that were sealed by the sacrifice of animal blood became null and void. To fill the vacuum that resulted, the prophets began to prepare the people for a new covenant.

The new covenant, which was sealed by the blood Christ shed on the cross, offers the unique hope of putting human lives back in order.

> Then, taking bread and giving thanks, he broke it and gave it to them, saying: "This is my body to be given for you. Do this as a remembrance of me." He did the same with the cup after eating, saying as he did so: "This cup is the new covenant in my blood, which will be shed for you" (Lk 22:20).

Fruitful participation in the celebration of mass is contingent on a

willingness to do what Jesus did after this meal, what he called his
"baptism."

> I have come to light a fire on the earth. How I wish the blaze
> were ignited! I have baptism to receive. What anguish I feel
> till it is over (Lk 12:49).

Baptism provides the foundation for celebrating mass by calling
for a commitment to plunge into the anguish that Jesus experienced as he suffered and died for our sins. The more willing we
are to allow our bodies to be broken with Jesus, and the more
willing we are to shed our blood with him, the more "holy" and
visible our communion becomes!

Jesus gave us the potential to put our lives in order and simultaneously started the fire he yearned for when he rose from the
dead; he continues to do so today as we use the power of the
Holy Spirit to overcome the effects of sin and death. The
tongues of fire that appeared on the first Pentecost ignited the
blaze that first made the church a light to the world. The Pente-
costal fire and light that were energized by the Holy Spirit are
still made visible by the closeness of our relationships to the
suffering, dying, and rising Jesus.

Through baptism and the eucharist, Jesus has given us what
we could never accomplish on our own, a relationship that is
both personal and "supernatural." Jesus, in teaching us to pray
to God as our "Father," used a word that is better translated as
"Pop" or "Dad"; this makes our relationship so familial that to
perceive sin only as the breaking of rules is to fail to understand
how close God desires us to be. By default, those who doubt
God's forgiveness instead perceive him as a punitive disciplinar-
ian. If their "e-*strange*-ment" continues, the supernatural grace
that they need will be choked off, and the force that separates
them from God and neighbor may even gather momentum.

Pride and sin separate us from God and strip us of the potential to have healthy relationships with others; this twofold alienation occurs when guilt causes us to:

1. attack others by projecting/shifting the blame from ourselves to someone else
2. attack ourselves by turning the anger inward—which causes either depression or physical illness

The cure for both of these human "dis-eases" is the spiritual unity that results from the sharing of unconditional love.

The uniqueness of human life lies in the healing and unitive power that can be generated by spiritual relationships. The commonality of the broken down and miserable relationships that characterize our time should serve as a warning that many in our society have lost touch with God. Spirituality is a life-giving vine, and when we are at our gracious best, God's eternal and unconditional love flows through that vine and into our lives, producing a unity that is so profound that words cannot describe it.

Salvation is a gift of relationship, with God, in the body of Christ. Its consequences are:

1. an extension of the "Word made flesh" event we celebrate as Christmas
2. an experience of the profound spiritual unity that exists only in the body of Christ

This extraordinary unity is the subject of the next chapter.

Table 25.1 summarizes this chapter by listing some of the characteristics that distinguish relationship from pride.

Table 25.1

From: Pride	To: Relationship
Other people are inferior	All God's children are equal.
Me me me . . .	Us
Mine	Ours
I'm	We're
Egotism	Sharing/teamwork
I'm religious/I go to mass every Sunday	I am fulfilling my baptismal commitment to suffer and die with Jesus.
Division	Salvation
Ownership	Stewardship
Control	Nurture
Blame others/project	Affirm
Poor self-image	Good self-image
Treat people as objects/use them	Empathy/compassion
It's not my fault.	Shared weakness
Destructive criticism	Constructive criticism
Self-exaltation	Humility
Suspicion/doubt	Trust
After all I did for you . . .	"It's better to give than to receive."
Judgmental	Non-judgmental
Energy depleting	Synergistic
Revenge	Forgiveness
Intolerance	Tolerance
Don't trust others	Most people are trustworthy
I know what's best for you.	What do you need?

CHAPTER TWENTY-SIX

ALIENATION
ALIENATION
ALIENATION
ALIENATION
ALIENATION
ALIENATION
ALIENATION

EXPRESS: ALIENATION?

UNITY
UNITY
UNITY
UNITY
UNITY
UNITY
UNITY

UNITY

OR   **UNITY?**

God has given us the wisdom to understand fully the mystery, the plan he was pleased to decree in Christ, to be carried out in the fullness of time: namely to bring all things in the heavens and on earth into one under Christ's headship (Eph 1:9–10).

Much of the alienation that is characteristic of modern life is the result of choices that exclude or even deny the existence of spiritual realities; the cure for the dis-"ease" that results is unity. This unity, which is born of relationships that reflect the Spirit of truth, leads inexorably toward the most profound human experience, love. Love is relationship. Relationship becomes unity. Unity becomes freedom. Freedom becomes truth.

Salvation is the experience of the spirituality of Christian love as the ultimate freedom, truth, relationship, and unity. See Figure 3.6.

Unity is the premier sign of our spiritual health because it fulfills God's plan to make Christ the focal point of life in heaven and on earth. Its significance is underscored by what Jesus was doing just before his arrest and subsequent trial before Pilate: he was praying for *unity.* He addressed the Father in these words:

> I pray that they may be [one] in us,
> that the world may believe that you sent me.
> I have given them the glory you gave me
> that they may be one—
> I living in them, you living in me—
> that their unity may be complete (Jn 17:21–23).

The closer we are to God, the closer we will become to one another; and the closer we are to one another, the more credible the good news of salvation becomes to non-believers.

Knowing that God wants us to become *one* in the body of Christ, we can begin to grasp his purpose. As Merton says in *The New Seeds of Contemplation:*

> If you really want to know what is meant by "God's will" in
> man's life, this is one way to get a good idea of it. "God's will"
> is certainly found in anything that is required of us in order
> that we might be united with one another in love.

"Love never fails" (1 Cor 13:8) because it is a *spiritual* choice, and because it is spiritual *it leads toward the unity that Jesus prayed for.*

The Acts of the Apostles describes the unity of the early church in these words: "The community of believers were of one heart and one mind" (Acts 4:32). Their mutual affection was the result of their willingness to try to share their gifts as generously as Jesus shared his. As Merton put it in *The New Seeds of Contemplation*, ". . . when you and I become what we are really meant to be, we will discover not only that we love one another perfectly but that we are both living in Christ and Christ in us, and *we are all one Christ.*" (Emphasis added)

The spirituality and lifestyle of the early church was based on three key elements: instruction, community life and prayer.

> They devoted themselves to the apostles' instruction and the communal life, to the breaking of bread and the prayers. . . . Many wonders and signs were performed by the apostles. Those who believed shared all things in common. With exultant and sincere hearts they took their meals in common" (Acts 2:42, 44a, 46b).

The celebration of mass in the Roman Catholic church is at the very center of our life as a community. We need to remind one another that to believe in "the real presence" at mass (belief that the bread and the wine become the actual body and blood of Christ) is also to believe in—and be convicted enough to practice—spiritual unity with God and neighbor. Receiving holy communion was never meant to be a private act. We eat of *one* loaf and drink from *one* cup to express our commitment to live in *one* body, the body of Christ, the church.

Thomas Merton in *The New Man* described the spiritual significance of unity in human relationships in these words.

> We are never fully ourselves until we realize that those we truly love become our "other selves." Seeing this, we are capable of beginning to grasp that God also loves us as He loves Himself. Without this awareness, there can be no perfect communion.

In the outpouring of our love for one another, the world is

supposed to see nothing less than the undiluted integrity of the body of Christ. Because the only direction this love can go is toward "heaven," our vocation is to embody its hope and healing power and thereby make its light visible here and now!

Sins become "mortal" or deadly by turning us away from God's life-giving Spirit. Sin and death are made up of captivity, illusion, pride, and alienation. Alienation of relationship in the body of Christ is to spirituality what death is to physical life. Its foremost symptom is anger. Anger is to spiritual life what pain is to our bodies. It is a warning, a reaction that is both healthy and necessary; it is *not* a sin in itself. *Anger is a symptom of a relationship that needs healing.* Those who repeatedly "confess" it as sin without making an effort to focus God's healing power on the situation that *causes* it face three dangers:

1. they will project/transfer the blame to someone else
2. they will hold the tension in—until they explode
3. they will turn the anger inward and become depressed

In all three cases, the result is an alienation that can only be healed by grace.

Physical death is inevitable; spiritual death is not. Physical death cannot touch our souls any more than our hands can touch a spirit. Sin is death; grace is life. Sin is darkness; grace is light. Sin destroys; grace creates. Sin alienates; *grace unites.* Amazing grace . . .

Table 26.1 summarizes this chapter by listing some of the characteristics that distinguish unity from alienation.

Table 26.1

From: Alienation	To: Unity
Sinfulness	Reconciliation
Competition	Affirmation
Conditions	Unconditional
Winning is everything	Grace is everything
"Keeping score"/getting even	Forgiving
Depression (anger turned inward)	Seek out and destroy the causes of anger
Hopelessness	Belongingness and love
Pessimism	Hope
Self-centered	God-centered
Confusion	Harmony
The pursuit of gratification	Spiritual life
Experience of sin as "mortal"/ deadly	"Mysticism" (grace is restoring the unity that existed before "Original Sin.")

CHAPTER TWENTY-SEVEN

Conclusion

A man found an eagle's egg and put it in the nest of a backyard hen. The eaglet hatched with the brood of chicks and grew up with them.

All his life the eagle did what the backyard chickens did, thinking he was just a chicken. He scratched the earth for worms and insects. He clucked and cackled. And he would thrash his wings to fly a few feet.

Years passed and the eagle grew very old. One day he saw a magnificent bird far above him in the cloudless sky. It glided in graceful majesty among the powerful wind currents, with scarcely a beat of its golden wings.

The old eagle looked up in awe. "What's that?" he asked.

"That's an eagle, the king of the birds," said a chicken. "He belongs to the sky. We belong to the earth—we're chickens."

So the eagle lived and died a chicken, for that's all he thought he was.

Until Pentecost, we had only "religion"; by God's gift of the

Holy Spirit, we are now able to share in the infinite richness of *spiritual* life. Spirituality is the fulfillment of baptism. Fulfilling the promise of baptism is to us what soaring is to an eagle. This is the adventure of faith.